Ann Lieberman
Lynne Miller

Teacher Leadership

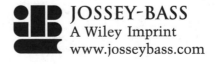
JOSSEY-BASS
A Wiley Imprint
www.josseybass.com

Published by Jossey-Bass
A Wiley Imprint
989 Market Street, San Francisco, CA 94103-1741   www.josseybass.com

Jossey-Bass books and products are available through most bookstores. To contact Jossey-Bass directly call our Customer Care Department within the U.S. at 800-956-7739, outside the U.S. at 317-572-3986 or fax 317-572-4002.

Jossey-Bass also publishes its books in a variety of electronic formats. Some content that appears in print may not be available in electronic books.

Readers should be aware that Internet Websites listed in this work may have changed or disappeared between when this work was written and when it is read.

Library of Congress Cataloging-in-Publication Data
Lieberman, Ann.
  Teacher leadership / Ann Lieberman, Lynne Miller.— 1st ed.
    p. cm. — (Jossey-Bass leadership library in education)
  Includes bibliographical references and index.
  ISBN 0-7879-6245-7 (alk. paper)
  1. Teachers—Professional relationships—United States. 2. Educational leadership—United States. 3. Teacher participation in administration—United States. I. Miller, Lynne, date. II. Title. III. Series.
  LB1775.2.L44 2004
  371.1'06—dc22   2004003236

Printed in the United States of America
FIRST EDITION
PB Printing 10 9 8 7 6

The Jossey-Bass Leadership Library in Education
Andy Hargreaves, Consulting Editor

The Jossey-Bass Leadership Library in Education is a distinctive series of original, accessible, and concise books designed to address some of the most important challenges facing educational leaders. The authors are respected thinkers in the field who bring practical wisdom and fresh insight to emerging and enduring issues in educational leadership. Packed with significant research, rich examples, and cutting-edge ideas, these books will help both novice and veteran leaders understand their practice more deeply and make schools better places to learn and work.

Andy Hargreaves is the Thomas More Brennan Chair in Education in the Lynch School of Education at Boston College and the author of numerous books on culture, change, and leadership in education.

For current and forthcoming titles in the series, please see the last pages of this book.

Contents

Acknowledgments

Ann would like to acknowledge the team at the Carnegie Foundation for the Advancement of Teaching who spent countless hours discussing teachers as leaders, trying to figure out how teachers' leadership is different from traditional leadership roles. The Carnegie teacher scholars who opened up their teaching lives to us made it possible for us to spend many hours not only supporting their scholarship but learning about the complexity of their work when they take on additional leadership responsibilities.

Lynne would like to acknowledge the team at the Southern Maine Partnership, its exceptional staff, the participating districts, and the wonderful educators who work in Maine to make schools respectful, caring, and challenging places for students and their teachers. The University of Southern Maine has been a hospitable host for the Southern Maine Partnership for twenty years and stands as an exemplar of how a university can collaborate with schools to the benefit of both.

We have been working together for many years, having written articles and books since 1984. It never seems to get easier, but it does get more gratifying. This book is no exception! Working with a collaborator can be a wonderful experience, but it can be frustrating too. How do two people develop one voice, one approach, and one set of ideas that cohere, while making use of the talents of two? This time we thought it would be a cinch, but like the other times, it was not. What is the right tone? What do we know? What do we need to know? How do we fit research and practice together? How do we talk about the impact of the changing world on teachers' work? Somehow, after lots of rewrites and lots of conversations, false starts, and continued work, we got it. We agreed on how to proceed and how to explain and describe what we knew about teacher leadership. And, as always, our respect for each other and our deep friendship rose above the disagreements and rewrites. Friendship, openness, and candor won the day, and we have produced another book.

We would like to acknowledge our loving spouses, who put up with us during that period while we struggled to get it right, and our children and grandchildren, who we hope will be recipients of the leadership of the kind of teachers we describe here.

ANN LIEBERMAN
LYNNE MILLER

The Authors

Ann Lieberman is emeritus professor at Teachers College, Columbia University, and a senior scholar at the Carnegie Foundation for the Advancement of Teaching. She is widely known for her work in the areas of teacher leadership and development, networks, and school improvement.

Her recent books include *Teachers Transforming Their World and Their Work* (with Lynne Miller) and *Inside the National Writing Project: Connecting Network Learning and Classroom Teaching* (with Diane Wood). Her many books and articles have helped to bring research to the field and also helped to popularize the perspective that learning in the field is another way of building knowledge about teaching and learning.

Ann's unique contribution is that she is able to go between school and university, embracing the dualities of education: theory and practice; process and content; intellectual and social-emotional learning; and policy and practice.

Lynne Miller is professor of educational leadership and co–executive director of the Southern Maine Partnership at the University of Southern Maine. Before moving to Maine, Lynne worked in Philadelphia as a high school English teacher and teacher-director of a public alternative school, in Boston as liaison to desegregation programs at Boston English High School, and in South Bend, Indiana, as both a high school assistant principal and associate superintendent for curriculum. An originating member of the National Commission on Teaching and America's Future, she continues to be involved in shaping teaching policy on the state and national levels. She has authored or coauthored numerous articles on teacher development, school reform, leadership, and teacher-constructed assessment and has collaborated with Ann Lieberman in writing or editing five books, the most recent of which is *Caught in the Action: What Matters in Professional Development*. Lynne views herself as "walking the fault line" between theory and practice. She is currently engaged in a large-scale high school transformation project in Maine and has particular responsibility for helping to develop pathways for underrepresented students who wish to attend college.

1

Why Teacher Leadership, and Why Now?

At a meeting in Texas in 2003 attended by teachers, novices, and veterans, we heard the following concerns:

- "We are showing numbers, not learning."

- "I am leaving teaching, because all the trust in teachers has gone. My voice and the voices of my colleagues were totally discounted as unimportant."

- "If your students don't score well, you are not a good teacher. That is what Texas has become."

- "Veteran teachers are leaving because there is so much stress. There is no relief from the pressure."

- "The atmosphere in my school is so negative. I know in my heart that this is wrong. I feel pain and loneliness. I don't want to give up. But I feel that I am being drowned by a huge wave."

How did we get here, as authors, as educators, as a country? What is going on in the world that is causing this angst, stress, and confusion in teaching, in learning, and in schools?

Changes in the World

Anthony Giddens, in his book *Runaway World* (2003), attributes the uneasy mood of the current age to fundamental changes that are on the order of the industrial revolution. These changes affect all aspects of our lives, including our schools. Of primary importance to Giddens is the growing tension between fundamentalism and cosmopolitanism. This tension reflects the disequilibrium that once-stable communities and nations experience when they are confronted with rapid and far-reaching economic and social change. In stark terms, this is a conflict between those who believe in a set of unchanging rules about how the world was created and how life should be lived, and those who welcome the variety and diversity that cultural changes bring to ways of thinking about and being in the world.

A case in point is the changing face of the family. In most industrialized countries, family structures are in flux. New ideas and practices about what constitutes a family challenge long held beliefs about the best way to raise children and organize domestic life. The traditional nuclear family is fast giving way to different configurations: single-parent families, families with more than one set of parents, families where both parents work outside the home, families where conventional roles are reversed, families where parents are of the same sex, families consisting of grandparents and their grandchildren, families of unrelated people who chose each other as kin. As the varieties of family structure multiply, the tension between fundamentalism and cosmopolitanism increases as well.

In the pages that follow, we explore how, as with families, converging forces in the world present a challenge to schools as they are currently constructed and understood. Dramatic shifts in the economy, government and public life, and demographics require cosmopolitan responses on the part of educators if public schools are to survive and endure.

Changes in the Economy

Globalization is the order of the day, leading to a new economy that depends on the production, application, and dissemination of knowledge rather than solely on the manufacture of goods and the provision of services. The new economy is fast changing the nature of work, shrinking the demand for manual labor and expanding the demand for knowledge workers. It encourages greater job turnover and career changes, "shifting career paths, serial careers and less loyalty" (Mazar, 1997, p. 19). Human capital and technology are central to this new world order, where a high school diploma is no longer a guarantee of a job or a career and postsecondary education is a necessity. The hierarchical bureaucracies that characterized the organizational life of most adults are being called into question; this creates confusion and imbalance. Competing expectations about how work should be organized have led some businesses to encourage team configurations and others to hold fast to traditional structures (Seely Brown, 1998).

Schools must accommodate themselves to the changing economic realities. In order to educate the workforce and citizenry of the future, they have to keep pace with marketplace demands as well as with technology and its effects on the way people communicate. People used to go to school because that is where the knowledge was (W. McIntyre, comments delivered at the annual conference of the New England Research Association, Portsmouth, New Hampshire, Apr. 2003). Now, public education has lost its monopoly on learning; almost anything can be found on the Internet. As schools compete with virtual academies and private providers for students, they have to make the case that they are better than their competitors at teaching people how to think critically, evaluate sources of information, and participate as full citizens in a democracy.

Changes in Government and Public Life

Globalization has also affected government and public life. The role of government has devolved in the last decade and continues to decrease in scope and influence. In efforts to increase efficiency, legislatures embrace the language, behaviors, and models of responsibility of the corporation. The adoption of a private sector ethos in the public domain has led to a view of government as a purchaser rather than a provider of direct services. The result is more support for privatization and increased subcontracting of public work to private, often for-profit agencies. "Management by results" has become the mantra of public administration, and with that comes the notion of the citizen as customer. Changing norms of public responsibility are evident in decreased public engagement, lower voter turnout, calls to cap taxes or reduce them, and a shifting of liability from the state to the family in meeting the needs of the young.

Schools have felt blindsided by the pressure to shift from public sector to private sector norms. Accountability schemes that depend on standardized measures of student progress and achievement are perhaps the most palpable effect of this new sensibility. The subcontracting of transportation and food service are less noticeable but equally indicative of the shift. Charter schools, magnet schools, home schooling, and vouchers for private education are all part of the agenda to reduce the role of government in what traditionally were considered public spheres. This shift presents schools with an enormous challenge: to figure out how to serve a public mission in a world that is increasingly comfortable with privatization of services.

Demographic Shifts

Demographics are also changing at a heady pace. Most of us are aware of the fact that the average age of the U.S. population is increasing. What is not so well known is that, at the same time, we are experiencing two consecutive baby boomlets, a flood of children who will enter school in record numbers. Mobility and transience are also on the upswing, playing an even greater role in population shifts than the growing birthrate. Schools will enroll proportionally more students who live in poverty, who come from diverse countries and ethnic groups, who represent different language and cultural backgrounds, and who enter with unequal social capital. This is the case for all schools, not just those in the inner city. As students migrate from the city to the suburbs, "Teaching in an inner suburb will increasingly resemble teaching in an inner city." (Hodgkinson, 2001). In addition, the increase in students with diagnosed learning disabilities will further affect schools, requiring them to provide a wide range of services and accommodations. If demography is destiny, then schools must be prepared to meet challenges that they have never before encountered.

The teaching force is also changing—in expected and unexpected ways. It stands to reason that an aging overall population, coupled with a boomlet of school-age children, will increase the demand for new teachers. What is unexpected is that retirement only accounts for one quarter of those leaving teaching in any one year (Stern, 2003). The large majority of teachers who leave the field do so for other reasons. Almost one third of teachers exit the field within their first three years; one half leave by the end of the fifth. The result is that for the first time in American history, the number of teachers leaving the profession is exceeding the number who are entering the profession. Tom Carrol expresses the urgency of the situation when he says, "It's become a crisis. We have a bucket with huge holes in it. They are leaving as fast as we can pour them in" (comments delivered in Milwaukee, Wisconsin, Oct. 2003).

Zumwalt and Craig (in press) warn that "increasing birthrates, immigration, teacher retirements and attrition are fueling the projected need for 200,000 new teachers annually over the next decade" and indicate that given this rapid turnover of teachers, there is legitimate fear that there will not be enough good teachers to meet the demands of the new century. It is predicted that by 2010 the United States will have replaced 75 percent of all current teachers. At the same time, there is legislation requiring that all teachers be "highly qualified" and meet demanding standards for certification and continued employment. The challenge to schools is daunting. They must recruit and retain an enormous number of new teachers in a very short time and provide them with the initial preparation and ongoing support for them to be successful. We have all heard too many stories in the past of inadequately prepared novices taking over classes in which knowledgeable teachers were desperately needed. We cannot afford to repeat these conditions for the next generation of students.

The Challenge for Schools

The major challenge for schools is this: ensuring that all students attain the skills, knowledge, and disposition they will need to be successful in the world that awaits them. The new economy demands that all students be prepared for work and for citizenry and that they all attain the high standards of achievement that have traditionally been reserved for a select few. This generation of students will need to graduate from high school with the ability to think and reason, a comfort with complex cognitive demands, a readiness to be flexible and adaptive, and a command of print, visual, quantitative, and digital literacies. This is a heavy load for schools, and it is compounded by the shifting demographics of the student population, the projected shortage of qualified and available teachers, and the reduced role of government in solving local problems.

There are two policy stances that have been developed in response to the challenge. There are policies that support standardization, accountability, and assessment and policies that support building capacity and enabling good practice. These contradictory views are not new; they are an integral part of our history and continue to influence our work today (Cuban, 1990).

Accountability Through Standardization

The most common policy stance is to hold schools accountable for meeting externally mandated standards of student achievement. The well-intentioned purpose is to establish a set of guaranteed outcomes for all students, to measure them objectively and efficiently, and to make the results transparent to the larger community. Unfortunately, the original intention has been diluted. Standards have become synonymous with standardized testing and have forced an alignment of assessments with narrow and reductionist curricula. Teachers are instructed to teach to the test rather than to the children. Transparency of results has been translated into sanctions against schools and students who do not meet standards in the required time and in the prescribed manner. In many instances, this undermining of original purpose is having negative effects on the ability of teachers to provide a rich and varied educational program for their students (Hargreaves, 1994, 2003).

In the mid-1980s, we saw the same rush to standards and testing, but for different reasons. In the United States, *A Nation at Risk* warned that declining student achievement, decreasing teacher knowledge, and lax academic and behavioral standards were a threat to the nation's economy and standing in the world (National Commission on Excellence in Education, 1983). In the United Kingdom, new tests for students at all grade levels replaced a system that was deemed inadequate for the new global era. The solution posited then was to mandate change, standardize curriculum, raise core requirements, and use tests to hold students and teachers accountable to policymakers and legislators. In the early 1990s, the U.S. Department of Education went so far as to consider implementing a standardized national test for all students (Lieberman, 1991). This initiative failed to become policy largely because of the efforts of the educational research community. Their arguments are worth repeating here. Researchers cited ample evidence that while testing tended to raise the low-level skills of U.S. students, it also led to the decline of higher-order cognitive skills because teachers tended to postpone teaching thinking and reasoning until after basic skills had been mastered for the required tests. The unintended consequence was that students in the lower tracks were exposed to a very limited curriculum that was oriented toward rote learning and drill and practice of the most rudimentary skills. These students never did well enough to get to the "good stuff" (Lieberman, 1991, p. 219). In effect, the teach-and-test policy increased rather than decreased the achievement gap. Darling-Hammond (1991) documented how the tests were being used for tracking and sorting purposes, systematically denying a group of students access to skills and knowledge while guaranteeing it to others. Using testing as a policy tool continues to have currency as a vehicle for improving student performance, even though it has proved ineffective and counterproductive in the past. There is another way.

Building Capacity and Enabling Good Practice

At the same time that *A Nation at Risk* was circulating in the United States, the Carnegie Corporation released a less heralded volume that offered a different perspective. *A Nation Prepared: Teachers for the Twenty-First Century* argued that imposing standards and tests was not enough to transform schooling (Carnegie Corporation of New York, 1986); rather, it called for the reinvigoration of the teaching force and a reinvention of the profession. It argued that teachers should become leaders in curriculum, instruction, school redesign, and professional development and that the real power to improve achievement lay with teachers, who needed to be entrusted with new responsibility and accountability for change.

A policy stance that enables rather than prescribes practice resonates with the central message of the Carnegie report. It is a viable alternative to "the widespread strategy of using mandates to legislate teaching practice[, which] assumes there is 'one best answer' to teaching problems rather than . . . a variety of approaches to teaching that are differentially effective in different circumstances" (Darling-Hammond and McLaughlin, 1983, p. 393). This kind of policy recognizes the knowledge and skills that teachers bring to their work and provides incentives to increase professional knowledge and to build on it.

As Darling-Hammond and McLaughlin (1983) suggest, the task of teaching diverse learners in pursuit of challenging goals is a complex problem that cannot be solved by top-down mandates and policies that promote standardization of means as well as ends. "It requires . . . the unmandating of conflicting policies as well as a new approach based on a coherent vision of teaching and learning across the school system and an appreciation of the diverse contexts within which teachers and students learn best" (p. 405). Policies that make sense in the context of teaching and that correspond with the needs and circumstances of teachers are a practical alternative to those that impose "standardized prescriptions for practice that impede teachers' ability to handle diversity" (Darling-Hammond and McLaughlin, 1983, p. 394).

Why Teacher Leadership?

In 1992 and again in 1999, we posed a set of propositions, or social system understandings, about teaching that were meant to characterize the realities of the profession from the teacher's perspective (Lieberman and Miller, 1992, 1999). We noted the following:

- Teacher isolation was the norm, leading teachers to develop unique repertoires of teaching strategies that were seldom shared or made public and often defended and protected.

- The reward system for teachers encouraged this isolation by placing responsibility for feedback on students rather than on colleagues and peers, allowing little room for public discussion and display of teaching.

- A weak knowledge base on learning contributed to individualism and privacy, requiring teachers to take on blind faith that what they were doing made a difference for their students; there were few supports for testing whether what teachers did mattered.

- Competing and conflicting policy directives reinforced these norms, so teachers created a personal rather than a shared sense of goals and expectations.

- The demonstration of control over student behavior functioned as an acceptable proxy for responsibility for student learning; control was visible, and learning was not.

- Teaching was a flat profession, requiring the same of neophytes and veterans and offering little support for professional growth and career differentiation.

- Teaching was construed as technical work to be managed, viewed as a prescribed set of skills, behaviors, and techniques to be mastered and evaluated.

We believed then, as we do now, that these realities keep schools from embracing the policies, beliefs, and practices that are necessary to meet the challenges of an ever-changing world. And we warned that as long as teachers were viewed as quasi-professionals rather than true professionals, they would work in schools that were trotting toward the future while the rest of the world was running toward it at full gallop.

Transforming the Social Realities of Teaching

It is clear that as a profession, we must refashion the old realities of teaching into new ones if we are to meet the demands of the new century. A new set of propositions about teaching that represent major shifts in perspective and practice has the potential to transform teaching and schools in the directions that the times require (Lieberman and Miller, 2000). These transformative shifts include the following:

• *From individualism to professional community:* When teachers view their work as taking place both within and beyond their own classroom, they participate in an authentic professional community. They build the capacity for joint work and develop norms of collegiality, openness, trust, experimentation, risk taking and feedback. Teaching becomes more public and more open to critique and improvement; in turn, the teaching community promotes an expanded view of professional responsibility and accountability—a move from concerns about *my* students in *my* classroom to *our* students in *our* school.

• *From teaching at the center to learning at the center:* When teachers shift their attention from the act of teaching to the process of learning, they corroborate for each other that "one size fits few" (Ohanian, 1999). By looking collaboratively at student work and designing curriculum, assessments, and instructional strategies together, they gain the collective knowledge, confidence, and power to co-construct alternatives to standardized approaches and measures.

• *From technical and managed work to inquiry and leadership:* When teachers cast off the mantle of technical and managed worker and assume new roles as "researchers, meaning makers, scholars, and inventors" (Lieberman and Miller, 2000), they expand the vision of who they are and what they do. They come to view themselves and are viewed by others as intellectuals engaged in inquiry about teaching and learning. Central to this expanded vision of teaching is the idea that teachers are also leaders, educators who can make a difference in schools and schooling now and in the future.

How Teacher Leaders Can Make a Difference

Teacher leaders are in a unique position to make change happen. They are close to the ground and have the knowledge and ability to control the conditions for teaching and learning in schools and classrooms. We believe that they are critical partners in transforming schooling. Among the many roles they can assume are the following:

• *Advocates for new forms of accountability and assessment.* Teacher leaders can challenge the dominance of tests as the sole criterion for success in school and offer alternatives to private-sector models of efficiency and accountability, introducing measures that promote learning, not just measure it. The call for accountability is not going to go away. Teachers as leaders are in a unique position to take hold of the issue and draw on their own experience and knowledge to enter the national conversation; they can help to reframe the public discourse from one that proposes an *accounting of learning* geared to an audience of legislatures and policymakers to one that supports an *accountability for learning* geared to an audience of parents and communities. In the final analysis, accountability schemes must involve teachers committed to taking responsibility for their own and their students' continual learning.

• *Innovators in the reconstruction of norms of achievement and expectations for students.* Teacher leaders can transform schools into communities that prepare students for citizenship and work in a complex, technological, and democratic society. The notion that only a select few are capable of achieving rigorous standards is no longer realistic or acceptable. The mantra that all children are capable of learning higher-order skills must be taken seriously. Teachers in leadership positions, whether formal or informal, can be important change agents in meeting the new demands that schools face. They can lead in reshaping the school day, changing grouping and organizational practices, ensuring more equitable distribution of resources, actively implementing curricula that are sensitive to diverse populations, upholding high standards for all students, and guaranteeing all can share in the full bounty of good teaching, materials, and support. In effect, teachers can lead a basic reconstruction of the very notions of ability, aspirations, and achievement.

- *Stewards for an invigorated profession.* Teacher leaders can work to support the profession and redefine it as an intellectual and collaborative enterprise. They can provide alternatives to restrictive mandates by expanding teachers' repertoire of strategies. They can advocate for recognition of accomplishments in teaching—for example, through candidacy for certification by the National Board of Professional Teaching Standards, teacher scholar positions, or mini-sabbaticals. And teacher leaders can lobby for meaningful professional development that draws on the experience, expertise, and wisdom of veteran teachers to support and inspire novice teachers and that promotes the creation of professional learning communities that sustain teacher commitment, passion, and persistence.

It is clear that in the last thirty years, the pendulum has been swinging between two polarities: policies that prescribe curriculum, instruction, and testing and policies that enable schools to build the capacity of teachers to seriously engage in transforming their school community. This book comes down strongly on the side of building capacity to engage in transformation. It is about teachers who take leadership in their schools, whether formally or informally, and learn how to turn educational policy into constructive practice. It is about building a new view of teaching and community. It is about building a professional ethos that respects diversity, confronts differences, represents a sensitivity to and engagement with the whole life of students and the adults who teach them. It is about teacher leaders who are creating learning communities that include rather than exclude, that create knowledge rather than merely apply it, and that offer challenge and support to both new and experienced teachers as colleagues. And it is about teacher leaders who make a difference.

2

What Research Says About
Teacher Leadership

.

Teacher leadership has been the subject of a good deal of attention and scrutiny in the past two decades. In this selective
review of the research, we focus on empirical studies as well as more
theoretical and interpretive work that we believe add to the knowledge base. To that end, we have found it useful to divide the literature into three broad categories or themes:

- *Individual teacher leader roles and organizational realities*: empirical studies of the roles individual teacher leaders play, what skills
the roles require, how these roles bump up against the structures and
norms of the bureaucratic school organization, and how teacher
leaders earn legitimacy within the school organization
- *Learning in practice*: descriptions of how teachers learn on the
job and in specific contexts to become leaders, interpretive accounts
of the nature of professional learning, and descriptions of how learning in practice is enacted in new teacher leadership roles
- *Teacher leadership and reshaping school culture*: descriptions of
broadened conceptions of teacher leadership, which place it at the
center of efforts to renew the culture in schools and build professional communities

Individual Teacher Leader Roles and Organizational Realities

Most of the early research on teacher leadership focused on individual teachers and the nature of the leadership they assumed, making only passing mention of the organizational context or wider school reform issues. In fact, Smylie (1995) reported that of over two thousand published articles on teacher leadership, most were descriptions of teacher roles and the organizational constraints that teachers faced in those roles.

Individual Teacher Leader Roles

In the 1980s, Miles, Saxl, and Lieberman (1988) studied teacher leaders in order to identify the skills and capabilities of faculty who had taken on change agent roles in three different reform efforts in a large city. The teacher leaders in the study had a broad range of abilities and experience before they assumed leadership roles, and they came equipped with a repertoire of effective interpersonal skills and an impressive array of academic credentials. They were knowledgeable about curriculum, because most had gained some experience in administrative and organizational pursuits. However, they quickly discovered that building collegial relationships was a complicated process; they had to acquire a new cluster of skills to help them gain acceptance from teachers and principals and to forge communications across role groups. The new skills included building trust and rapport, making an organizational diagnosis, using resources, managing the work, and building skill and confidence in others. The teacher leaders also came face to face with the social realities of teaching in most school organizations and came to see, with new insight, how isolated teachers were and what this isolation did to them.

Wasley (1991) performed an in-depth study of three teacher leaders, each with a different focus, geographical location, and role.

Her study revealed that these leaders, despite their disparities, shared common problems: difficulty in working within bureaucratic systems, lack of incentives for teachers to assume new roles, and teachers' resistance to becoming involved in reform efforts. Wasley concluded that in order for teacher leadership to become a reality, teachers must be given real support for their work. Further, she suggested that school culture be altered to accommodate these new roles. Whereas the Miles, Saxl, and Lieberman study pinpointed the skills and abilities that teachers developed, Wasley's research got at the dynamics of leadership as it was practiced over time. She offered an inside look at teacher leadership that demonstrated both the obstacles and the potential for teachers who reached out beyond their classrooms.

Teacher Leadership and Organizational Constraints

Descriptions of new roles for individual teacher leaders and how they negotiated school organizations were helpful to a point. But questions remained. What caused conflict? Ambiguity? Discomfort? Burnout? Or even success? Wasley raised some of these very issues, and a new group of researchers explored them further. Their research started with the recognition that teachers performed their leadership in the context of their schools, and it looked to the organization as the stage upon which the work was accomplished. The research found that the bureaucratic, hierarchical nature of schools often conflicted with the collegial nature of the reforms that teacher leadership was designed to bring about. The researchers concluded that structures endemic to schools made it difficult for teachers to become authentic leaders.

Focusing on organizational elements, Smylie and Denny (1990) documented the certainties and uncertainties associated with the roles of thirteen teacher leaders in a district. They described how these leaders adjusted to the tensions and ambiguities in their roles as well as to the organizational factors that supported or constrained their new work. They found that although teachers were supported by the district and were knowledgeable about classroom practice, they were uncertain about their role within the organization—whether other teachers knew or understood their work as teacher leaders or whether the expectations of the principal regarding their role matched their own. Smylie and Denny uncovered tensions about the proportion of time to be spent on classroom responsibilities versus leadership responsibilities and how the role of teacher leader related to the principal's role. Smylie and Denny concluded that organizational factors, such as the lack of time to adequately perform their leadership functions, made it difficult for teachers to perform the new tasks assigned to them.

This organizational perspective helped explain why some teacher leaders suffered role conflict and ambiguity and found it difficult to do their jobs: not only were they trying to support change and build collaborative relationships, but they were also taking on the traditional bureaucratic and institutional norms of the school. There were powerful organizational forces at work that either supported or thwarted teacher leadership.

The Quest for Legitimacy

Little (1995) explored the question of organizational legitimacy for teacher leaders when she documented the evolution of leadership in two secondary schools in the process of restructuring. She identified two key issues: "contested ground" and leadership legitimacy. She also found that teacher leaders were caught between strategies of commitment and strategies of control. According to Little, when teachers advance a restructuring agenda, they must work toward collaboration, experimentation, and flexible use of time and space within an environment that also supports the bureaucratic controls of evaluation and curriculum alignment. This becomes the "contested ground," the ground between the two opposing forces that operate in the school and on the teachers. Teachers who lead must somehow learn to negotiate between these two forces and move their school forward despite the strong pulls to maintain the status quo. In secondary schools, Little reports, it is subject matter expertise that gives teachers their legitimacy to lead.

Bartlett's study of teacher leaders in two schools further explored the concept of "contested ground" that Little had uncovered (Bartlett, 2001). She examined two reforming schools, both of which supported teacher leadership. One school, although it allowed powerful teacher roles, lost much of its leadership because teachers found that they could not teach and lead at the same time. The demands of the two roles took too great a toll on their personal and professional lives. The will and the support for teacher leadership were there, but the structures, time, and distribution of work were not. In the other school, there were better provisions for teacher leadership, but ancillary tensions intruded on the lives of teacher leaders. Bartlett's study graphically illustrated how the absence of appropriate structures and culture make it difficult for teacher leaders to negotiate reasonable personal and professional lives.

Little and Bartlett (2002) referred to this dilemma as "the Huberman Paradox," an acknowledgment of the work of Michael Huberman, an international scholar who looked at teacher careers over time and across continents. Huberman (1993) found substantial differences between the lives of teachers who ended their careers with a sense of serenity and satisfaction and those who exited with feelings of disenchantment and bitterness. The teachers who were most content spent their years in teaching tinkering at the classroom level. Those who were most bitter spent their time engaging issues at the school and district levels. The paradox is this: on one hand, teachers were stimulated by their involvement in reform work and leadership in their school; on the other hand, that very work led to burnout, disaffection, professional conflict, and disappointment (Bartlett, 2001).

Spillane, Hallett, and Diamond (2003) also studied how teachers assumed leadership roles and gained legitimacy within the school organization. Using observations of eighty-four teachers in Chicago's elementary schools, they found that teachers constructed others as leaders based on the interactions they had with them. As a rule, teachers valued subject matter expertise in other teachers and were most comfortable assigning leadership roles to peers who demonstrated a certain level of expertise. Unlike principals who came by their leadership through formal organizational positions, teachers who were subject matter experts became leaders because they had accrued the cultural, social, and human capital necessary to lead within the school. The work of Spillane and his colleagues articulated a clear path to teacher leadership within the organizational confines of a school.

Miller and O'Shea (1991) documented other paths toward teacher leadership. In their study of four teacher leaders in one elementary school, they uncovered four diverse warrants for leadership: (1) *leadership through experience:* a veteran teacher is acknowledged as a leader by virtue of her time in the system and her reputation as a classroom teacher; (2) *leadership through knowledge:* a relative newcomer is granted authority by "dint of her intelligence, her driving curiosity, her search for new knowledge, and her power as a classroom teacher" (p. 202) to transform theory into practice; (3) *leadership through vision:* a midcareer teacher is valued for his ability to imagine new ways of assessing, displaying, and communicating student progress and his willingness to involve others in making his vision a reality; (4) *leadership through respect for children:* a librarian invents a role for herself and is awarded credibility as an advocate for tying student self-knowledge to academic learning through her visible and direct work with children and through presenting demonstration lessons in classrooms. Like Spillane, Hallett, and Diamond, Miller and O'Shea concluded that teachers come to leadership informally through the construction of peer interactions. They also found that "each teacher followed a unique trajectory, . . . each led from a particular strength, . . . each was rooted in classroom practice. . ." (1991, p. 209). Legitimacy was earned, not granted.

Learning in Practice

A second body of scholarship focuses on how teachers learn their new roles and how to enact them. Researchers from fields outside of education were the pioneers in studying professional learning and how it occurs. They began with the observation that professionals learn by actually doing the work and reflecting on it. Gawande's description of how surgeons learn their craft stands as an apt description of such a process. Reflecting on one of his first surgeries, in which he couldn't get it right, he reported, "In surgery, as in anything else, skill and confidence are learned through experience—haltingly and humiliatingly. Like the tennis player and the oboist and the guy who fixes hard drives, we need practice to get good at what we do. . . . We want perfection without practice. . . . Learning is hidden, behind drapes and anesthesia and the elisions of language" (2002, pp. 18, 24).

Gawande's account resonates with the ways that teachers learn to become leaders: on the job, through experience and practice, by trial and error, seldom visible and often hidden. Although they are taught theories and skills in preparation for their work, teacher leaders learn most of what they need to know in the process of performing the work. The concept of learning in practice is now viewed as foundational to teacher leadership; it rests on the idea that learning is more social, collaborative, and context-dependent than was previously thought. In the next two sections, we explore the roots of this concept and its implications for understanding how teachers learn to become leaders.

Theories of Reflective Practice and Situated Learning

Schön (1983) laid the foundation for understanding learning-in-practice when he coined the term *reflective practice*, which is now commonplace in the literature, as a starting point for developing a theory of learning in the professions. For Schön, learning took place on the job, where people developed "theories in use" that were derived from their own experience in practicing their craft. He argued that professionals did not apply knowledge; they created it. Often spontaneous and sometimes chaotic, the process of reflective practice allowed people to uncover what they already understood and knew how to do—what Polanyi (1967) had called "tacit knowledge"—and to build on that knowledge by making it more explicit so that it could expand learning and deepen practice. Learning, in this view, was not the transmission of knowledge from an expert to a novice; rather, learning was discovery. It made the private public and the implicit explicit (Schön, 1991, p. 5).

By situating learning within specific professional settings, Schön opened the door for educational researchers to examine the development of teachers' learning as it occurred under different conditions and to explore the connections between learning and context. By focusing on what teacher leaders actually did in different settings, researchers were able to develop understandings about why teacher leaders encountered difficulty within bureaucratic organizations and assumed leadership roles with more ease in smaller learning communities. In the first instance, leadership responsibilities were considered an add-on to an already heavy teacher workload. In the second instance, teacher leadership was supported by the provision of adequate time, space, and resources and by the establishment of responsibilities that fell within a reasonable set of expectations. In the learning community settings, teachers assumed leadership as part of their work, not in addition to it.

Professional Learning Within Communities of Practice

Lave and Wenger (1991) added to the idea of learning in context. Their social theory of learning rests on three processes—learning, meaning, and identity—that occur side by side in communities of practice in which social practices are espoused and enacted. "Learning is both social and collective, rather than individual and social" (Lave, 1996, p. 149) and comes about by social participation. It cannot be designed; it happens through experience and practice. In plain terms, people learn from and with others in particular ways. They learn through practice (learning as doing), through meaning (learning as intentional); through community (learning as participating and being with others); and through identity (learning as changing who we are).

Borrowing from Schön, Wenger (1998) views practice as both explicit and tacit, including both what people say and observe and what is left unsaid and begs for explanation. It includes "subtle cues, . . . untold rules of thumb, . . . sensitivities, embodied understandings . . . and shared world views" (p. 47), as well as a community willing to share the work publicly. Central to learning in communities of practice is "the construction of identities" (p. 280) within a community of practice where newcomers can absorb "how masters of their trade talk, walk, work and generally conduct their lives; how people who are not part of the community of practice interact with it; what other newcomers are doing; what newcomers need to learn to become full practitioners; increasing understanding of how, when, and about what old-timers collaborate, collude, and collide and what they enjoy, dislike, respect, and admire" (Lave and Wenger, 1991, p. 98). Professional learning so constructed is rooted in the human need to feel a sense of belonging and of making a contribution to a community where experience and knowledge function as a part of community property. "Such participation shapes not only what we do, but also who we are and how we interpret what we do" (Wenger, 1998, p. 4).

Hargreaves (2003) deepens our understanding of communities of practice when he compares them to what he calls "performance sects," approaches that he characterizes as valuing results over process and viewing learning as transfer rather than as the making of meaning and identity. In their efforts to train teachers to master standardized scripts and externally imposed rules, performance sects deny them the authority that comes from the joint construction of knowledge that occurs in a community of practice.

Learning new roles within such a community requires what Lave and Wenger term *legitimate peripheral participation* (Wenger, 1998). *Legitimate* refers to the rightful place that is accorded the newcomer by the full-fledged members of the community. *Peripheral participation* refers to the stance that the newcomer assumes. Neither a full participant nor an uninvolved observer, the newcomer has the advantage of rehearsing new roles and taking risks in a community of support and assistance. Thinking of professional learning as a legitimate and peripheral form of participation for newcomers is a significant shift.

Rogoff (1994) commented that such a perspective offers an alternative to both the teacher-centered and student-centered approaches that have dominated the discourse about learning. In this new iteration, neither the teacher nor the student has the strong authority position; instead the community is responsible for the learning of its participants. This helps to explain why learning to lead is eased for teachers who are part of professional communities and why it is more difficult for teachers who function individually within their school organization. Moore (2004) states, "It turns out that organizations, in and of themselves, may be poor settings for learning. . . . The very glue that organizes a group of people—roles, responsibilities, norms, and procedures—limit the feedback and errors that lead to learning. To learn, the practitioner must have a place 'in the balcony' from which to watch the action, critique the performance, and reflect on what needs to be done next. That is why collegial relationships and networks of practice are invaluable to the ongoing development of the school leader" (pp. 87–88).

Teacher Leadership and Reshaping School Culture

The third body of literature that we will consider explores broadened conceptions of teacher leadership and views teacher leaders as engaged in the work of reshaping the culture of schools. It focuses on teacher leadership roles that involve the reconstruction of relationships and meaning, the transformation of conditions for teaching and learning, and the development of an ambitious new view of the profession.

Teacher Leadership and Reculturing Schools

In 1995, Fullan wrote about the necessity of extending the notion of teacher leadership. He advocated moving away from a narrow view of a single individual trying to make a dent in a bureaucratic system toward a more complex perspective that involves multiple levels of leadership, all engaged in reshaping the culture of the school. Working together as a cohort rather than as individuals, teacher leaders can build a new collaborative culture. Such a culture would have the capacity to support the diverse leadership approaches and configurations necessary to "reculture" a school (Fullan, 1995).

Fullan mapped the professional work of teacher leaders by identifying six domains of teacher leadership work: knowledge of teaching and learning, knowledge of collegiality, knowledge of educational context, opportunities for continual learning, management of the change process, and a sense of moral purpose (Fullan, 1994, p. 246). It was clear that no one person could assume all that leadership required. In order to be enacted, teacher leadership had to be shared. Fullan's expanded notion of teacher leadership not only lifted the burden from individuals but also provided the criteria for distributing the professional work of leadership throughout the teaching force in a school.

Lambert (2003) also wrote persuasively about broadening the concept of teacher leadership. She offered a view of "constructivist leadership," which is grounded in "relationships, community, learning and purpose" (p. 14).

She saw the concept of leadership as being in transition, in line with Fullan's notion of "reculturing." In Lambert's articulation of leadership, it is not a role but rather "performing actions . . . that enable participants in a community to evoke potential in a trusting environment; to inquire into practice; to focus on constructing meaning; or to frame actions based on new behaviors and purposeful intention" (p. 13). Under this definition, many people in an organization or school could perform acts of leadership. Leadership, understood broadly, could build an environment for the continual learning and participation of the adults as well as their students.

Both Fullan and Lambert pointed to a new direction in understanding and supporting teacher leadership. They replaced the limited vision of teacher leadership as an individual enterprise trapped in existing school organizations with a broader conception of teacher leadership as groups of teachers intentionally working together to transform the very cultures in which they work and lead.

Teacher Leadership as Building Community

A view of teacher leadership that is closely related to reculturing schools encompasses building a professional community. McLaughlin and Talbert (1993) first used the term *professional community* when they reported on a five-year study of secondary schools in California. They found high school departments where such communities existed, in which groups of teachers talked openly about their students and the problems they were having, discussed curricular and pedagogical approaches to making changes together, taught one another different strategies and practices, and committed themselves to collective discussion and action with their peers as colleagues. These high school departments were in sharp contrast to the norm of loose collections of teachers who each worked alone.

Westheimer (1998, p. 12) further defined community as involving interaction and participation, interdependence, shared interests and beliefs, concern for minority views, and meaningful relationships. In his now-classic study of two middle schools, Westheimer further refined his concept of community. Both schools had strong professional communities but were unlike in kind and culture. The forms of participation and interaction differed in each school, as did the ways that members expressed shared interests and handled conflict and minority opinion. The first school, "Brandeis," was a community that was tied together by respect for individual rights and differences. The other school, "Mills," was ". . . driven by a strong collective mission and collective values" (Westheimer, 1998, p. 120). Brandeis teachers looked within their own community of teachers and sought support from one another; Mills teachers extended themselves externally and gained support from the larger community. Professional community for Brandeis was procedural and conforming. For Mills, it was characterized by joint work, broad leadership responsibilities, and strong identification with the larger community.

Westheimer drew several lessons from his study. First, beliefs matter. The Mills teachers believed in a communal ideal; the Brandeis teachers believed in individual rights and innate abilities. The differences in beliefs permeated the culture of the school. Second, structures matter. The Mills teachers developed structures that encouraged innovation. Their structures tended to support a culture of participation. For Brandeis, there were fewer structures for both participation and conflict; Brandeis teachers developed forms for participation, which Hargreaves (1994, p. 195) calls "contrived collegiality," that were imposed, required, and ordered rather than developmental, integrated, and part of the life of teachers. Westheimer's study uncovered how professional communities can differ in their cultural commitment to participation, shared visions, and ways of working together.

Little (1990) analyzed the conditions under which teachers acted as colleagues within a community and described how they move from independence to interdependence. She developed a continuum that began with storytelling and scanning (the occasional opportunistic contacts that teachers have), moved to aid and assistance (giving help and advice) and then on to sharing (exchanging materials, strategies, and ideas) and finally to joint work (collective action based on shared responsibility such as an interdisciplinary team). Her analysis demonstrated that an authentic professional community in schools tended to develop over time with increasing levels and complexity of teacher engagement and was powerful in changing the norms of privacy.

Grossman, Wineburg, and Woolworth (2001) conducted a three-year study of a large secondary school that illustrates the pangs of developing a professional community. The research focused on what happened when twenty-two teachers from the English and social studies departments participated in a book group that was created specifically for the purpose of building community and studying it at the same time. Community was defined as providing for the learning of students and the learning of adults. As the teachers worked through the "inevitable conflicts of social relationships, and formed structures to sustain relationships over time" (p. 3), they confronted the cultural and vocational impediments that were involved in building a community across traditional boundaries. The study documented the dynamics of the growth of a community from its inception and identified a number of fault lines of conflict among the teachers. Conflicts arose over differences in disciplines, gender and racial differences, and difficulties in learning to work and learn together. The researchers also uncovered a lack of capacity to do what they termed the "social work" of building a community and the necessary social norms of genuine civil discourse. This study presented a powerful narrative of how a professional community is formed. It described the dynamics of beginnings and the evolution from subgroups and factionalism to a mature community through the exposure and working through of differences. It highlights what it takes for teachers to persist and learn to take responsibility for their own growth and that of others.

Promising New Teacher Leadership Roles

The shifting conception of teacher leadership is represented in research that documents three promising new roles: teacher as researcher, teacher as scholar, and teacher as mentor. Teacher as researcher derives from a genre of research that creates new knowledge from direct teacher practice and reflection rather than from more removed methods of observation and interpretation. As a form of leadership, teacher research attends to both process and results and leads to improvement in classrooms that can extend to the whole school. The seminal work of Cochran-Smith and Lytle (1993, 2001) describes how teacher research and inquiry not only leads to an articulation and improvement of individual work but also influences the school culture. Because it generates knowledge that is local, contextual, and immediate, it resonates with the dilemmas of practice that other teachers experience. Teacher research is a form of reflective practice. It not only creates new knowledge, allowing teachers to see their practice in a new light and improve on it, but it also makes inquiry a critical component in teacher learning and school redesign.

Teacher as scholar builds on the idea of teacher as researcher and expands it (Shulman, 2000). The Carnegie Foundation for the Advancement of Teaching, in a program known as the Carnegie Academy for the Scholarship of Teaching and Learning (CASTL), expands the idea of teacher research to include scholarship as a central tenet of the work of teaching. Scholarship is characterized by the necessity of making one's work public in some form, being amenable to having it critiqued, and passing it on to others so that they can build on it. CASTL researchers found that when teachers studied their own practice and made it publicly available to others, they felt far more efficacious about their teaching and they approached their peers in substantially different ways.

When leadership has scholarship at its foundation, it is more about expertise, credibility, and influence than it is about power, authority, and control. Teacher scholars influence others by collaboratively studying practice, reading other researchers' work, and making their own work available as a source of discussion and action by their colleagues. They promote learning-in-practice for others as they enact it for themselves (Hatch, Eiler, and Faigenbaum, 2003).

Teacher as mentor or coach is another leadership role that allows teachers to make their work public and assist in the reconstruction of the profession. It is important to note that the terms *mentor* and *coach* have been appropriated by some of the "performance sects" that Hargreaves (2003) describes. In those instances, mentors and coaches work from predetermined scripts to transmit the one right way or the "best practices" that authorities, who are far removed from the context of particular classrooms, have established and sanctioned. Strong and St. John (in press) report on a project in which mentors assume a more complex and ambitious role as guides for new teachers and as agents for reculturing schools.

The Santa Cruz New Teacher Program, which developed under a statewide initiative, releases veteran teachers from classroom responsibilities to serve as full-time advisers to groups of fourteen beginning teachers. The program has been very successful in easing the entry of new teachers into the profession and in keeping them: 94 percent of the 1992–93 and 1997–98 cohorts of newcomers were still in education after six years—89 percent in teaching and 5 percent in other roles (Strong and St. John, in press). Just as important, however, is the program's emphasis on creating systemwide norms and practices that promote career-long learning and inquiry into practice. To that end, the program engages advisers in their own induction program. Here they learn and practice the skills as coaches, classroom observers, and group facilitators that they need to be effective with their advisees. With strong links to administrators and to the participating sites, the program for mentors doesn't leave them to fend for themselves; it ensures that they learn their new roles as members of communities of practice, and it also prepares them to confront organizational realities that affect new teachers in particular and their own teaching and the teaching profession in general.

Originally conceived as a form of teacher empowerment, teacher leadership has earned its place in the professional literature. It has grown in sophistication and complexity over time. The studies reviewed in this chapter demonstrate an unfolding of descriptions, interpretations, and theories that began with stories of individual leaders striving to "make a dent" in the school organization, moved on to analyses of how new organizational roles were learned and enacted, and culminated in new conceptions of the role and its possibilities. When taken together, the research provides a foundation for understanding the power, promise, and perplexities of teacher leadership.

3

Learning to Lead in Communities of Practice

I n the previous chapters, we laid the foundation for understanding the contemporary context for teacher leadership and for appreciating the scholarship that defines its practice and possibilities. Here, we want to demonstrate how the research is enacted in real life, how teacher leadership is built and sustained within professional communities of practice. We describe two such communities that build teacher leadership. The first is the National Writing Project, a thirty-year-old national network that develops teachers of writing who are also teachers of teachers and school leaders. The second is Leadership for Tomorrow's Schools, a regional collaborative that grows teacher leaders for its schools and districts.

Both the National Writing Project and Leadership for Tomorrow's Schools are living examples of Wenger's (1998) communities of practitioners. They are "arenas for professional learning because people in them imbue activities with shared meanings, develop a sense of belonging, and create new identities" (Lieberman and Wood, 2003, p. 21). Both organizations enact the tenets of professional learning within a community of practice: learning is experiential and collective; it is context-driven and context-sensitive; and it occurs through social participation. Though different in their stated goals, structure, and activities, both the National Writing Project and Leadership for Tomorrow's Schools rely on a set of social practices that promote learning, meaning, and identity and that assist teachers in coming to view themselves as teacher leaders and in learning to act the part.

The National Writing Project

The National Writing Project (NWP) is about to celebrate its thirtieth birthday. While it is unknown in many quarters, the NWP ranks as one of the most successful professional development efforts in the United States and is arguably the most ambitious. It has over 175 sites and has built a core of over four thousand teacher leaders, called "teacher consultants," who play a variety of leadership and teaching roles in their schools, districts, and states and within the National Writing Project network (Lieberman and Wood, 2003). The teacher consultants learn to lead literacy efforts in their classroom and in their school as they participate in the NWP. The organization of the network, the social practices it creates, the supports for leadership it provides, and the role it assumes in the transformation of professional development are all intertwined.

The NWP is best understood as a network of educators in which professional development in literacy instruction is intentionally seeded with opportunities to build teacher leadership in literacy development. Teachers learn to become better instructors of writing and, in so doing, establish the authority to lead others. With a strong foundation in both research and practice, the NWP builds a community of practice and simultaneously builds leaders. The story begins with the summer invitational.

The Summer Invitational

The Summer Invitational is the heart of the National Writing Project; it is a five-week institute involving twenty to twenty-five teachers, all of whom have applied and been selected to attend as NWP fellows. Across the country, teachers involved in the NWP leave their home schools and familiar environments and come to college campuses; the idea of a school-university partnership is central to the NWP. The institute involves the fellows in a collegial community that develops over the course of an intense time together. It engages like-minded educators who care about teaching, improving their practice, and better serving their students. Most important, it brings teachers together in an enterprise that is intentionally social and collective rather than individual and isolated, in which caring and knowing are equally valued. Three activities form the core of the institute (Gray, 2000): forums in which teachers teach one another, opportunities for teachers to read and discuss relevant educational literature and research, and response groups in which teachers write and share their writing with one another. Following is a conflated description of what occurs at a typical institute.

On the first day of the institute, the site director introduces the concepts of authorship and audience, which are central to the writing project. Authorship and audience involve participants in the process of generating an idea, revising it, and making it public to an audience. Wood and Lieberman (2000) note, "Becoming an author requires the ability to draw from imagination, to create, to set purposes and intentions and to act on them. It requires the stamina to articulate, assess, revise, entertain feedback, assess, edit and publish one's ideas. And authorship requires ownership" (p. 262).

The director teaches a carefully prepared writing lesson, replete with handouts and instructions, to the audience of fellows, who assume the role of students. At the end of the lesson, participants are asked to complete their first writing task: penning a letter to the director that tells her what they liked about the teaching strategy, what could be improved, and how they might use such a strategy in their own classroom.

Later in the day, the director takes the "author's chair" and reads a short story that she is writing to the fellows, who now function as a critical audience; they are asked to help deepen characters, clarify the action and the plot, and so forth. The director will come back with a revised version of her story several times during the institute. Each participant will have opportunities to sit in the author's chair during the course of the institute. The movement between being an author and an audience not only provides opportunities for writing and responding to writing but also builds a community of practice among members.

In the afternoon, participants read children's books together and talk about how they might be used. There is also a discussion about a piece of research and its relevance, led by a former participant. Food is ubiquitous, and conversation flows freely.

At the beginning of the second day, the leader reads from a log she kept of the previous day's activities. From then on, teachers will take turns serving as the official logger of each day's events and will read from the log at the beginning of the next session. By the end of the day, teachers have engaged in two major activities that will sustain them for the five weeks of the institute: teaching a strategy or lesson and participating in writing groups, in which they will continue to function as both author and audience, produce four pieces of writing in different styles, and respond to the writing of others. Someone has volunteered to bring food, an indication that leadership is passing from the director to participants, who are learning to take care of the community. By carefully crafting an infrastructure for learning, the institute builds a professional community. The community dignifies the happenings of the previous day, surfaces and acknowledges the practical knowledge of teachers, promotes collegial feedback and critique, and engages people in reading and critiquing research. It is also develops the potential for leadership. The fellows come to terms with their own expertise; they have the opportunity to experience and practice the responsibilities of teacher leadership; they learn to make their teaching public and open to critique; and they become skilled at bringing other teachers together to share their knowledge and to co-construct their professional learning.

By the fifth week, teachers are invested in the topics that they and others are pursuing; they have begun to build a habit of professional reading; and they have become sensitized to what it takes to produce a piece of writing that is of high quality, having written and revised many times with the help of their writing groups. For many participants, the institute is the first time that they have seen and experienced what it takes to participate in and build a learning culture that is led by and supported by teachers. They learn to become better teachers of writing by writing and by demonstrating their practice to others; at the same time, they gain experience in participating in groups where critique, support, and encouragement to improve are the norms. In the process, many teachers find that they like teaching adults in this way and that the expression "starting where the learners are" is as applicable to their peers as it is to their students. Institute graduates, who are called teacher consultants, bring these understandings home. They play a vital role in the institute: coaching teachers in planning demonstration lessons, sharing their own research and that of others, and providing information about regional and state concerns. More important, they model leadership in literacy development and provide a glimpse of the opportunities for leadership beyond the classroom that await the fellows at the end of the summer.

As the institute draws to a close, the fellows have deepened their ability to communicate in writing, to talk about learning and teaching, and to invest in ideas and unpack theories. These are skills that not only promote better writing and writing instruction but also are foundational to becoming effective teacher leaders.

Learning and Leading Beyond the Institute

Teachers who experience and internalize the social practices of the Invitational are not only prepared to be better teachers of writing but also prepared to be teacher leaders. They return to their classrooms and schools in a new role: "When teachers graduate from the summer institute where they were 'fellows,' they become 'teacher consultants.' This nomenclature is a way of reminding teachers they have the capacity to play a public role in serving the profession." (Wood and Lieberman, 2000, p. 269).

The teacher consultants form a cadre of teacher leaders who work on local, regional, and national levels under the umbrella of the NWP. They are equipped with theoretical and practical knowledge about how learning takes place; they know the research on literacy development and have the capacity to unpack the research for others; and they have a repertoire of ideas, not a box of recipes. The teacher consultants play a variety of roles. They participate in and often direct "continuity programs" under the auspices of the local site. These programs provide opportunities for teacher consultants to stay connected as members of a professional community and to engage in ongoing development as teachers, learners, and leaders. Continuity programs may include book groups, writing groups, workshops and advanced institutes, or opportunities to publish teacher research.

Teacher consultants also have opportunities to direct in-service institutes in districts and schools. For example, a district may decide that it wants to focus on writing for a semester or a year. The district contacts the local NWP site and negotiates a contract in which a teacher consultant is assigned to the district as a consultant and compensated from district funds.

In addition, teacher consultants engage in activities at the national level. For instance, if the national office is interested in pursuing a grant, it may call on teacher consultants from across sites to come together and collaboratively craft the grant proposal.

Finally, as indicated earlier, teacher consultants play a substantial role in the summer institutes, where they model good teaching and good leading in literacy development.

In all of these leadership roles, teacher consultants depend on the National Writing Project for assistance and support. In effect, the NWP establishes an infrastructure that weds professional development for improved classroom practice with professional development for school leadership. In so doing, it consolidates good teaching practice as well as leadership across the sites, ensuring its own viability and durability as a network in the process.

Social Practices That Support Learning and Leading in the NWP

In a community of practice, learning does not take place as the result of a fixed curriculum as much as it occurs through a "field of learning" that exists exclusively in the social practices of the community (Wenger, 1998, p. 100). The field of learning in the Invitational centers on learning to write "the NWP way." This engages teachers in reflecting first on their own practice; presenting their work to a group of colleagues; getting feedback in the form of critique, support, and suggestions for improvement; and, finally, encouraging others to think about how they might use the ideas that have been presented. This process creates avenues for both teacher development and leadership development. It asks individuals to go public with their work, have it scrutinized by their peers, improve it, justify its use in relation to a local or statewide set of standards, and present their teaching to an audience of adults. Over time, NWP members learn that their own practices are worth sharing, sometimes worth emulating, and always worth improving. Their hard labor is dignified (rather than discounted), and their participation is sought (rather than silenced). This is the stuff of teaching; this is the stuff of leadership.

In their study of the NWP, Lieberman and Wood (2003) identified the social practices of the NWP:

- *Approaching each colleague as a potentially valuable contributor.* Everyone who comes to the institute is viewed as having something of value to contribute. It is this acceptance that helps people risk going public with their practice and their writing. It is not that everything is acceptable, but that starting where people are is the way people build on their learning.

- *Honoring teacher knowledge.* Teachers commit themselves not only to teaching what they know but also to learning from others. They gain knowledge about the subtleties of their own and others' practices, and in the process, they become more articulate about teaching, students, and curriculum. By gaining pride in the knowledge that they have collectively created, they view themselves and their profession differently.

• *Creating public forums for teacher sharing, dialogue, and critique.* A critical part of the summer institute is learning to go public with one's work. In preparation for playing a more public role, teachers learn the give and take of criticism from their professional peers. They learn from their own public performances that collegial critique is essential. And they grow to internalize the community norms of listening, critiquing, and self-critiquing as well as asking questions of practice.

• *Turning ownership of learning over to learners.* Teachers learn that they can take charge of their own learning and that they do not have to be passive consumers of knowledge from external sources. They develop internal accountability systems that are far more effective than standardized measures in monitoring and assessing progress. All the practices of the NWP place teachers' knowledge at the center.

• *Situating human learning in practice and relationships.* Professional learning happens through reading, listening, participating, and doing things with others. As practice deepens and relationships develop, teachers are more likely to take risks and to seek and accept critiques and suggestions from their peers. Over time, teachers rely on opportunities to practice their craft in the company of others as an essential ingredient in their own development and that of others.

• *Providing multiple entry points into the learning community.* Whatever the reason that teachers choose to become part of the NWP and whatever their philosophy or ideological preference, they are welcomed into a professional community that values pluralism and embraces knowledge from both inside and outside the network. The community has an egalitarian flavor and embraces dualities and contraries rather than a single truth; this is the opposite of a one-size-fits-all approach. All that is required is a willingness to work with others, to care for the group, and to embrace the dilemmas of practice.

• *Guiding reflection on teaching through reflection on learning.* The institute begins with reflections on learning and moves to what these reflections mean for teaching. As the fellows become teacher consultants, they have the opportunity to explore what reflection means in leading the learning of others. As part of the NWP, teachers spend a great deal of time reading, listening, and discussing what they are learning and what it might mean for their classroom and school. Unlike traditional professional development, this approach emphasizes knowledge and habits of mind over technical skills. Participation, reflection, and practice constitute learning rather than direct instruction on what is often glibly termed "best practice."

• *Sharing leadership.* In the summer institute and beyond, teachers observe and practice new norms of leadership. They take turns teaching one another, serving as one another's presenter and audience, organizing and participating in one another's groups, and sharing in one another's practice. They learn that leadership is powerful when all members of the community take an active part in sharing it. Teacher consultants who choose to pursue leadership beyond the institute do so by internalizing the social practices that are practiced daily during the institute.

• *Promoting a stance of inquiry.* An inquiry stance is far different from a solution stance. It requires that one ask questions of one's practice rather than look for answers. It places contextual data collection and analysis rather than generalized solutions at the center of improvement efforts. It helps teachers internalize the idea that learning to teach is a lifetime affair. An inquiry stance recognizes, legitimizes, and celebrates the potential of all teachers to change lives.

• *Reconceptualizing professional identity and linking it to professional community.* By making connections between content and teaching within a viable professional community, NWP participants are able to forge new professional identities that are rooted in collaboration, collective knowledge and practice, and joint ownership of exciting ideas, struggles, and strategies. Teachers come to the institute as solo players and return to their schools as members of an entire orchestra. This community helps generate energy, participation, and intellectual stimulation.

While these ten social practices are indigenous to the National Writing Project network, they also can represent a broader view of what is entailed in a community of practice: they ensure social participation; foster learning, leading, and learning to lead; and constitute an infrastructure for sustained growth and deepening practice. Lieberman and Wood (2003) conclude:

> The social practices adopted by the NWP convey norms and purposes, they create a sense of belonging, and they shape professional identities. The teachers we saw enacting the social practices of the NWP surrendered reliance on routine and conventional teaching approaches in order to continuously search for better ways to meet students' needs and they saw themselves as conducting the search not only as individuals but also as members of a professional community. . . . It is important to emphasize that these practices are interactive and mutually dependent. And that together they have the power to generate teaching cultures very unlike those of typical schools. [pp. 21, 22]

Leadership for Tomorrow's Schools

Leadership for Tomorrow's Schools (LTS) is another example of how teachers learn and practice new roles within the context of intentional communities. Like the National Writing Project, it is based on the principles of professional learning discussed in Chapter Two. Unlike the NWP, it involves participants in two communities simultaneously: a two-year cohort group that crosses district and school boundaries and an ongoing leadership community that is located within the sending district. This second community is where participants practice and perform their leadership work.

The idea for a new way to build leadership emerged within the ranks of the Southern Maine Partnership (SMP), a school-university collaboration that is housed at the University of Southern Maine and that has as its mission the redesign of schools and educator preparation in behalf of student learning and equity. In 1997, a subset of SMP superintendents decided it was time to, in their words, "grow our own leaders." Dissatisfied with the university's traditional leadership preparation program, which they viewed as a series of ungrounded and disconnected courses, the superintendents asked the SMP director to invite university faculty to co-design an alternative. They wanted an approach that was better suited to the demands and challenges that schools were facing and would be facing in the future. Planning began on an island in Casco Bay, where a group of public school educators, university faculty, and business leaders spent two days together. Using a planning backward model, they developed a list of descriptors that distinguished "the schools we have from the schools we need." They then set about developing a program to prepare leaders for the schools they envisioned.

Core Commitments

LTS planners agreed to develop a two-year program of experiences for district teams of teachers, all of whom were to be selected by their superintendent on the basis of leadership potential. They reached consensus that neither effective teaching nor effective leadership alone had sufficiently affected the conditions for student learning. They concluded that both were essential. The LTS planners also agreed that neither schools nor universities, working on their own, had been successful in building effective leadership. They subscribed to the view that in order to build new leadership, each type of institution would have to draw from its strengths, acknowledge its weaknesses, and work to complement the other. What emerged from the planning retreat was the outline of a program that would be designed based on desired ends rather than prescriptive means and that would join academic courses and real-life work, focusing on essential questions about teaching, learning, and leading. Participants would enroll as members of a district team and move through the program as a distinct cohort over a period of two years. The program would require that school districts and the university forgo "business as usual" and create new ways to advance school leadership.

Now in its third iteration, the LTS program links learning and leadership through university and district work and rests on a set of commitments from all involved:

• Teacher participants commit to remaining in the program for the full two years, working in district and cross-district teams, taking leadership roles in the district while in the program, attending eight full-day classes and eight evening classes, completing all assigned work, and working alongside district mentors throughout the program.

• District superintendents commit to selecting LTS participants, ensuring meaningful district work opportunities, providing eight full days of released time for participants and paying for substitute coverage, reimbursing all course tuition, identifying appropriate mentors, and attending three seminars designed for superintendents.

• University faculty commit to co-designing and co-teaching all courses with district personnel, holding all courses in a location that is easily accessible to participants, combining course content across areas to ensure a seamless academic experience, designing performance assessments that connect academic work and district work, leading superintendent seminars, and using the LTS model to redesign traditional university leadership programs.

While the core commitments remain constant, the organization of program elements changes with each new cohort. Following is a description of how the LTS program is organized and enacted for its third cohort.

The First Year

The first year is framed by this essential question: How do we know when effective teaching and learning occur? The large portion of leadership development takes place in the cohort community. The year begins with an introductory meeting in the spring that brings together alumni from the first two cohorts with new participants, along with district superintendents, university faculty, and school principals. This is a time to review the planning document's description of the difference between "the schools we have and the schools we need" and explain the purpose of the program, the commitments for all involved, planned activities, and expected outcomes. Program alumni take center stage, describing LTS and its effects on them as well as the impact they have had as leaders in their schools and districts. The presence of the superintendents conveys a message about the degree of district investment in the leadership development of participants. The university faculty members review the sequence of courses and the connections they will make to practice. A convivial meal and excited conversation conclude the introductory session.

Participants, who represent all grade levels and subject areas, come together again in the fall for the first day and a half of classes, which meet on Thursday evening and all day on Friday once a month. The first-year sequence of classes combines work in teaching and learning, assessment, and observation and supervision— content that is traditionally taught as three separate graduate courses at the university. In LTS, the academic work is divided into modules, each lasting four class meetings and each building on the previous ones. Each module is team-taught by university and school-based faculty. In the first module, participants view a tape of teaching episodes and discuss them. They quickly realize that they do not have a common vocabulary for talking about teaching either within or across districts and schools. Next, they read research about effective teaching and assessment and then return to the taped episodes, demonstrating to each other the power that comes from a shared vocabulary and knowledge base. In small and large groups, they come to terms with the gaps in their knowledge and practice and set goals for themselves. In the process of reading, discussing, and observing, participants reflect on themselves as students and as teachers; sometimes they come to recognize how disconnected learning must seem to their students.

The next module introduces a set of skills for giving and receiving feedback on observations of teaching. Participants watch and then practice a cycle that involves preconference, observation, and postconference; in the process, they draw on the vocabulary of teaching and assessment that they now share. During the year, pairs of teachers complete a cycle of three observations in which they both observe and are observed. The observation cycle becomes the centerpiece of the year's work, serving as both a springboard for and a mirror of the reading and research in which participants engage. Superintendents provide time for the observations to occur within the school day. Each course session also schedules time for teachers to provide feedback to each other and to assess their progress.

The year continues as a dialogue between research and practice and between ideas and skills. Participants work in district and cross-district groups, seeking to make sense of and develop personal meaning from their collective experiences. They experiment with small leadership projects in their schools and work with existing teacher leaders; they review district policies on teaching, assessment, and teacher evaluation; and they meet monthly with their superintendent. During the year, the superintendents come together for three seminars that are led by LTS faculty, who offer an overview of the academic work of the course modules.

The first year ends with each team preparing and making a presentation to its district administrator. This is the first real step that LTS participants take into the leadership community of their district. The presentation involves an analysis of district policy and practice in light of the experience and knowledge gained through LTS. In addition, each team member develops a contract with the superintendent and the principal that details the leadership work each will undertake in the fall. The superintendents and LTS faculty meet over the summer to design the academic and practical work that will constitute the second year. While the focus for the second year has already been set, the form and specific content have yet to be established. This depends on the collaboration of partners and the co-construction of syllabi and experiences.

The Second Year

The second year centers on this essential question: What kind of leadership is necessary to create and sustain an organizational culture and enabling structures that promote learning? As in the first year, cohort members meet monthly for coursework. And, as in the first year, traditional university course delivery systems are replaced by modules that create a seamless fabric of experience, practice, and learning. The content focuses on professional development, organizational behavior, and leadership and reflects the thinking of the school-university teams that met over the summer.

In the second year, leadership roles become more formalized and expand from school to district work; participants spend a large portion of their time doing assigned district leadership tasks. The mentoring component is established, and participants begin meeting as regular members of the district administrative team. In addition, cohort members complete a formal analysis of their district's organizational culture and how it supports or impedes teacher leadership. All of the work flows from a heightened awareness of issues surrounding teaching, learning, and assessment and how the culture of the school affects the conditions of learning for both students and teachers. The second year ends with an exhibition and celebration to which district administrative teams and teaching colleagues are invited; participant teams present summaries of their collective engagement in LTS and how it has contributed to the work of their district and to their personal development as leaders. Team members also present their plans for how they will continue to work together and what individual and joint leadership tasks they hope to tackle.

Learning and Leading Beyond the Cohort Program

Graduates of LTS greet the new crop of candidates the next fall, just as they were greeted two years before. Most of the alumni elect to apply the course credits they have accumulated through LTS to a graduate degree, which is arranged through an articulation agreement that was completed during the planning stage of LTS. Some graduates aspire to administrative positions, but most want to continue in their role as a teacher leader. For this group, the district becomes the major venue for ongoing leadership development and professional growth. As fully participating members of their district leadership community, LTS graduates assume a variety of roles: elementary grade-level leader, middle school team captain, high school adviser, mentor for new teachers, school or district coordinator of curriculum or assessment, grant writer, facilitator of professional development, or mentor to new LTS participants. A few decide to apply for certification by the National Board of Professional Teaching Standards; those who are successful then lead others through the process.

Social Practices That Support Leadership Development in LTS

The organizing idea of leadership development in the LTS program is legitimate peripheral participation, "the process by which newcomers become included in a community of practice" and learn how to become full participants in and practitioners of new roles (Wenger, 1998, p. 100). In applying the concept of legitimate peripheral participation to the second cohort of Leadership for Tomorrow's Schools, Moore (2004) has identified six key social practices that form the foundation for learning to lead in the program:

- *Having legitimate access to a community of school leaders.* LTS participants are nominated by their superintendent, mentored by their school administrators and other teacher leaders, and provided authentic leadership tasks to complete for their district. As members of two communities of leaders, they have frequent and regular access to school leaders in monthly cohort meetings and in their district and school leadership teams as they become involved in leadership tasks.

- *Engaging in the practice of leadership, first in peripheral ways and ultimately as full participants.* The two-year program is structured to provide graduated entry into the sending district's community of practicing leaders. Peripheral involvement as an observer, as a student of school culture, and as an investigator of practice evolves into more substantive participation as a member of a district team involved in authentic leadership tasks. By the end of the two years, participants have completed a major leadership task and have regularly attended leadership team meetings.

- *"Performing" the practice of leadership.* Participants have many opportunities to act as leaders, to "perform" leadership, throughout the program. In the first year, they perform leadership in the observation cycle, in small leadership projects with other team members, and in the end-of-the-year presentation to their district leadership team. In the second year, opportunities to perform leadership increase. Participants are assigned actual leadership tasks, for which they are fully responsible; they attend leadership team meetings; they work alongside their mentor; and they make presentations to a variety of audiences.

• *Fostering identity as leaders and the motivation to lead.* Because of the nominating process, participants are aware from the beginning that they are expected to wear the mantle of leadership in their school and district. Being a member of an LTS cohort signifies that an individual has leadership potential and that the district is willing to make an investment in realizing that potential. As leadership opportunities deepen over the two years of the program, so does one's identity as a leader.

• *Helping district leadership to change.* At the end of each year of LTS, participants make a formal presentation or exhibition to the district leadership team. The focus of the first year is on reviewing policies and practices that affect teaching, learning, and assessment and on bringing forward a healthy critique as well as new ideas. The second year's focus is on policies and practices that affect organizational health, professional development, and district planning and goals.

• *Participating in the reproduction of the community of school leaders.* The LTS experience extends beyond the two-year formal program. When participants leave that portion, they may become fully participating members of the leadership community in their district. In that role, they engage in the renewal of existing structures and the generation of new leaders. They welcome the new cohort of LTS; they serve as mentors to participants; they oversee initial leadership projects; and they recommend new nominees for the program to their superintendents.

The LTS experience and its social practices provides LTS participants with legitimate peripheral participation in their district leadership community; eventually, districts gain full members in their leadership community.

We conclude with an excerpt from an interview with one LTS participant:

> This has been an unbelievable two years of personal learning about education, teaching and learning, sys-

tems, leadership, and communication. Being exposed to others who had experience as teacher leaders helped me figure out the structures that allow teacher leadership to be effective. Everything from running a good meeting to doing advance work with skeptics became part of being effective. The experience has made a huge difference in my life. Most important has been having the opportunity to share assumptions, developing a common language, being involved in joint inquiry, finding a direction for my work, learning to craft a framework from shared learning, and seeing how to use existing resources to build capacity to get district work done.

4

Portraits of Teacher Leaders in Practice

This chapter focuses on the work and lived experiences of four very different teacher leaders from two very different states. We have chosen to write about people and contexts that we know, so that we could present rich descriptions of the work they do and how they do it, the beliefs and assumptions they hold, the ways they work with their colleagues (both veterans and novices), and the particular struggles they face within their particular policy environment. Two of the teachers, Yvonne Hutchinson and Sarah Capitelli, are from California and have been participants in the Carnegie Academy for the Scholarship of Teaching and Learning (CASTL) K–12, with Ann Lieberman and Tom Hatch as codirectors. The other two teachers, Gerry Crocker and David Galin, are from Maine and have worked alongside Lynne Miller in regional and statewide initiatives.

Leading in California

California educates one in eight students in the United States, having grown in population from just over four million in the 1940s to

Melissa Eiler-White's unpublished doctoral dissertation, "Going Public: The Travel of Teacher Research" (Stanford University, Stanford, Calif., 2004), was very helpful in understanding Sarah Capitelli's practice and the importance of inquiry in her work as a leader.

over thirty-four million in the year 2000. The general population has become multiethnic and multiracial, and this is reflected in a school population that now draws on fifty immigrant groups and at least as many language clusters. The consequences of this tremendous growth, along with large-scale political and social change, have been enormous for K–12 education.

Once the bellwether for educational excellence, California has been in decline for over thirty years. Three events share responsibility for this downward spiral. First, in 1968, the case of *Serrano* v. *Priest* challenged inequities between school districts in spending on schools. Second, a tax revolt culminated in the passage of Proposition 13, which severely reduced the amount of money available to schools through property taxes. Third, in 1998, voters passed Proposition 227, which essentially ended bilingual instruction in the state. These three policy initiatives added to the state's shortfall in resources and services available to all students, but particularly to those most in need of language development and other supportive programs.

In the last five years, California schools have lost the music, art, physical education, library, and summer programs that were long considered part of the school system. Facilities, many built over fifty years ago are in grave disrepair. Hundreds of students are taught in portable buildings and makeshift rooms, many of which are unsuitable for learning. All of these conditions are especially burdensome at a time when schools are expected to teach all students and hold them to higher standards.

The prescriptive policy response in California has created new dilemmas for the teaching profession.

- Legislation was passed to reduce class size in the first three grades. This brought thousands of underprepared teachers into the system and placed them in schools where students were most in need of expert teaching.

- The Public School Accountability Act of 1999 called for the creation of standards at the state level that were mandated to guide all local curricula. The Academic Performance Index (API) was the cornerstone of the act; it provides a rating of schools that is based predominantly on their scores on mandated state tests, among them the California High School Exit Exam, which qualifies students for the diploma. The Statewide Testing and Reporting System (STARS) collects, manages, and reports the data from the testing. In response to the act, many large urban districts adopted rigidly standardized reading programs that limit teacher professional discretion and devalue their experience and expertise. It is within this context that Yvonne Hutchinson and Sarah Capitelli teach and use their classroom teaching as a springboard for leading their colleagues in collaboratively solving the issues they face daily.

Yvonne Divans Hutchinson: Connecting Teaching, Learning, Leading, and Living

Yvonne Divans Hutchinson is an active member of the National Writing Project and is certified by the National Board of Professional Teaching Standards. An NWP teacher consultant since 1978, she has held various teacher leader roles over the years. She is part of a literacy cadre and coordinates teachers from across the disciplines who are interested in literacy development; she provides professional development and support as needed. A resource teacher in her district, she also serves as a curriculum coordinator, literacy coach, and cochair of the English department. Last year, she conducted all of the staff development at her school and was an official mentor for new teachers. She was a member of the second cohort of CASTL scholars and recently served as a National Board of Professional Teaching Standards scholar and an instructor at the University of California, Los Angeles, and for the Los Angeles Unified School District.

In all of these roles, Yvonne holds fast to a set of principles she learned as a young woman growing up in the segregated South in the 1940s. Her commitments and passions grew from the guidance of her mother and other African American women who encouraged her intellect and her love of reading and nurtured her as a young girl. She learned early to love reading and to care passionately about humanity. This same spirit pervades her ninth-grade classroom in South Central Los Angeles and her work as a teacher leader. For Yvonne, it all begins in the classroom.

The Context and Character of Yvonne's Classroom

Yvonne teaches English at King/Drew Magnet School for Medicine and Science, which serves a largely minority population that is 72 percent African American and 22 percent Latino. As a teacher, Hutchinson's main concerns are that her students become good human beings, learn to appreciate the diversity in their classroom and the world, and become good readers and writers. Her teaching, which combines the two big ideas of literacy and diversity, was equally influenced by Martin Luther King's statement about the importance of the "content of their character" and Alice Walker's comment: "I imagine good teaching as a circle of earnest people sitting down to ask each other meaningful questions. I don't see it as a handing down of answers." Love of literature and learning to work with others regardless of their race, class, or ethnicity dominate the community that Hutchinson builds in her classroom. Recognizing the strong oral tradition of African Americans, she builds on this strength, even as she works to reduce the gap between her students' oral expression and their reading and writing:

> I have made oral and literate discourse strategies a centerpiece of my high school English curriculum. I draw from the rich oral traditions of my African-American and Latino students and encourage them to use their oral

skills to investigate rigorous literary texts to engage themselves and each other in substantive discussions about controversial issues. [Hutchinson, 2003]

On the first day of class, students come in and sit by their friends, dividing themselves along racial and ethnic lines; Hutchinson chides them about doing so. She turns her back and asks them to rearrange themselves so that they can learn more about each other and about life outside the classroom. This is the beginning of her efforts to raise the level of her student's social attitudes, honor their talents, scaffold their learning, and develop their habits of mind. Her humor, warmth, and compassion make this first move possible, so that students can begin to learn racial tolerance as well as how to read, discuss, and critique literary texts. This, along with mutual respect and decency, are built into classroom work.

Hutchinson believes that thinking about texts and participating in discussions about literature are essential skills: "Thinking with text is where I begin with my students: avid readers, indifferent readers, struggling readers, functionally illiterate readers" (Hutchinson, 2003). Her goal is to create literate discourse in the classroom. Drawing from her experience with students who are reluctant to participate in discussion, she has developed a protocol with stock responses that provides them with a language that they can use in discussion.

> To ensure that everyone, especially the most reticent student, speaks up in class, I require at least a one-sentence reply whenever someone is called upon in class discussion. The ground rule is that everyone must speak, if only to demur. And if a peer calls on another, the student must respond with a cogent answer. S/he cannot demur. The students learn stock responses so that everyone develops the habit of engaging in discourse. During

discussion, which is usually open-ended, students are encouraged to express their ideas, thoughts, and opinions, and to justify them with evidence and logical reasoning. Students who are bereft of ideas momentarily may resort to the stock responses that appear below. Since we understand that everyone needs varying lengths of time to think, members of the class will sit quietly and wait for a response from their more reticent classmates. They might even coach him/her to make the appropriate response. [Hutchinson, 2003]

Sample stock responses include the following:

I don't know, but I will try to find out the answer and get back to you.	when you don't know the answer
I don't know.	when you are confused
I regret to say that I am not prepared.	when you haven't done the homework or are unprepared
Please come back to me; I'm still thinking.	when you are having difficulty coming up with an answer
I do not wish to share this time, but I will be happy to share next time.	when the discussion is of a personal nature or you don't want to participate

Yvonne has also developed a procedure for ensuring that all students have an equal voice in discussion and the opportunity to practice using oral language publicly. She calls on the first person, who then calls on someone else who is different in gender, race, or ethnicity. She also uses controversial issues to engage students in oral communication. For example, in a unit on corporal punishment, students read the section of *Black Boy* by Richard Wright in which he is beaten by his mother for lighting the house on fire. They then read two articles from newspapers that reflect differing views of punishment. Students then complete a comparative analysis of the three pieces and hold a whole-group discussion in which they relate the pieces they have read to their own lives.

In addition to helping her students learn how to think about texts and participate in classroom discussions about them, Hutchinson builds in opportunities to use creativity in oral expression. Every day a scribe reports on the previous day's work. In this way, every student has the opportunity to practice the rigor of thinking, working, and participating with others; they are encouraged to be creative in their oral report of the previous days' activities. By carefully scaffolding the learning and participation of her students, Yvonne creates a safe environment where students feel that they are learning to be in the world as they are learning to be students of literature. That Yvonne has been successful in achieving her two goals of enhancing character and increasing literacy is reflected in the comments of her students:

> The instructor's humorous discussions . . . made us feel like we were at home, learning on our own. I actually felt the connection with everyone. . . . The mixture of races . . . made me feel more comfortable around other races. Working together made the class fun. [Daniel, tenth grade]

> I have now become an avid reader, thanks to (my teacher) introducing me to such writers as Walter Dean Meyers, Richard Wright, Terry McMillan, and many more. . . . I have grown a hunger for reading books, just as Richard Wright did. [Jamelle, ninth grade]

Connecting Classroom Practice to Teacher Leadership

What makes teacher leadership at once so intriguing and so slippery is how closely it is tied to classroom practice and the ability to articulate what one does and the questions that it raises. Yvonne's leadership is tightly coupled with her commitment to her students' learning, participation, and overall development. Having thought about, written about, and nuanced her practice, she never leaves the role of teacher behind; she takes it with her when she organizes, mentors, and engages other teachers as a leader among peers. She maintains her passionate commitment to developing civility and literacy. Her leadership practices with adults clearly reflect her beliefs about teaching, her embracing of difference, and her growing confidence and willingness to go public about her practice.

Beliefs and Practices

Hutchinson views leadership in the same way that she views teaching: not as handing down information but as creating a circle of people who come together to share and learn from one another. Her approach is always to model participation, build habits of mind, and support people in becoming apprentices to their own learning. She often shows her colleagues how she teaches: how she engages students in a variety of learning activities, how she encourages the development of their own voice, and how she places student work at the center of her teaching. By demonstration rather than remonstration, she allows others to see that it is possible for all students to achieve, no matter what their social, economic, cultural, or educational circumstances. Through civil discourse, she engages teachers in conversations about their practice. Rather than judge teacher complaints about students, she redirects them by asking such questions as "What would you like to see?" By putting the responsibility back on teachers, she encourages them to better understand their own motivations and commitments to their students. They, like her students, find their own voice.

Yvonne also engages teachers in telling stories of possibilities that are rooted in real practice. She encourages teachers to talk about their own work and build new strategies that enlarge and deepen their repertoire. Hutchinson recognizes that it is important to see authentic possibilities and understands that teachers, like students, need opportunities to actively engage in their own learning instead of being told what to do. While she is herself learning, she leads others by encouraging them to reveal to themselves and others what they are doing. She asks teachers to use the new and nuanced ideas they learn from one another to build on what they know about their own teaching—sometimes discarding, sometimes expanding, sometimes experimenting.

Respecting Difference

Yvonne understands that in leadership, as in classroom teaching, she has to vary her approach for different audiences. Veterans and those new to the profession have different needs. Like all students, they require differing approaches to learning.

Novice teachers appear to be more open and appreciative of opportunities to learn how to engage their students than more experienced teachers, but they need a boost of confidence. As students of their own practice, they appear to be more deferential and tentative than other teachers, but they are eager to do well and join in the collegial conversation. Avoiding the usual "sage on the stage" stance, Hutchinson shows what she has learned and how she continues to learn from her students by modeling her own inquiries about her practice. New teachers are excited about seeing strategies and approaches to literacy development and engagement and often try to emulate what they see. Hutchinson inspires and invigorates novices through her gentle and deeply thoughtful approach to her students and to her subject matter. Their comments of "I can't do it!" and "I'm no good" are met by Hutchinson's asking them to identify their strengths and begin a conversation about possibilities that can be tried. She offers numerous strategies from the context of her own work.

Veteran teachers need to approach new ideas in very different ways from novice teachers. Veterans already have a repertoire of strategies that they have developed over time. Their interest lies in refining or adding to their repertoire. Sometimes they surface mandated needs for participation. Veteran teachers often start with

"What else can I do? I tried this and it didn't work; what else can I do?" Hutchinson often begins by stating that she doesn't have the answers and then encourages teachers to use the opportunity to work together to share what they have developed. By including student work and student voices, she demonstrates how she constantly works to figure out the best ways to encourage learning. Hutchinson leads by modeling the kind of engagement with peers that she has with her students. When she models participation in her own learning, she inspires veteran teachers to share what they are doing. As teachers engage in a conversation with others, they come to replace their negative attitudes toward students with strategies for engagement and participation.

Yvonne is effective with veteran teachers because she takes her own learning seriously. She is supported by a group of colleagues in her school who meet regularly to inspire each other with success stories, swap ideas, and figure out how to fix the trouble spots in their teaching. In these collegial conversations, both new and veteran teachers meet as friends to celebrate teaching, to exchange teaching ideas, and to affirm and confirm the wonders of teaching for each other. For further support, Hutchinson has several close friends who honestly share stories about all that is happening in their classroom. They provide mutual support, friendship, and guidance through the complexities of their teaching lives because they are connected by close friendship, respect for one another, and a love of teaching.

Going Public

A major aspect of Yvonne's persona, one that distinguishes her as a teacher leader, is her willingness and courage to go public with her work and to encourage other teachers to do so as well. Her Web site, called "A Friend of Their Minds: Capitalizing on the Oral Tradition of My African American Students," reflects the love of literature and the belief in humanity that characterize all of her work (http://gallery.carnegiefoundation.org/yhutchinson).

> The title comes from a passage in *Beloved* by Toni Morrison, in which Paul D. tells Denver about Sethe, her mother, saying, "She was a friend of my mind." I love that idea, and I think it captures the essence of my relationship with my students. [Hutchinson, 2003]

The site, which was developed when Yvonne was a Carnegie scholar, opens her classroom and her teaching to a wide audience; it makes her private classroom visible and her implicit assumptions explicit. The site includes teacher narratives about "thinking with text" and "question-answer relationships," four videos (one instructional segment; what can be learned from the Web site; a reflective interview with Hutchinson; and interviews with students), and strategies for promoting literate discourse (including the stock answers). But the Web site is much more than the table of contents indicates; it is a revelation of how a teacher thinks, plans, revises, and reflects. Yvonne's Web site shows the power of going public and also demonstrates the confidence, competence, and commitment of an individual who models what she espouses as a teacher and as a leader.

In all of her leadership work, Yvonne shows rather than tells, respects rather than prescribes, and engages in authentic conversation rather than lectures. Valuing community building, Hutchinson finds ways for teachers to contribute to their own work and that of their colleagues. These are the same values that drive her classroom instruction.

Sarah Capitelli: Leading Informally Through Inquiry into Practice

Sarah Capitelli is a relatively new teacher, now in her fifth year of teaching at Melrose Elementary School in Oakland. The school's population is 79 percent Latino, 12 percent African American and 5 percent Asian American students; all of the students that Sarah teaches are English language learners. Melrose has a reputation for taking its bilingual program seriously; it offers a sequence of experiences that begins with Spanish as the primary language and gradually progresses to full English instruction by the fourth grade. The school is a long-standing member of the Bay Area Coalition of Equitable Schools, which supports classroom-based teacher research. Teachers are regularly involved in research, both independently and as members of collaborative inquiry groups.

Sarah's leadership emerged from her concern for the English language learners whom she taught and from her developing interest and expertise in teacher research:

> Since beginning my teaching career, I have been concerned with how to best meet the needs of my English language learners during English language development class. In particular, I am concerned with how to help them create a strong foundation for their learning of English.

Sarah was first introduced to methods of inquiry during her first year of teaching, when she attended a series of professional development offerings given by Bay Area IV, a regional professional development consortium. While doing this, she was being mentored by Anna Richert, a well-respected teacher educator from Mills College who is known for her focus on inquiry into practice. As a student at Mills, Sarah had learned from Anna that inquiry is an important part of what it means to learn as a teacher. Her professional development experience, in combination with the Mills program in which she was involved, created a sense that inquiry was an important part of a teacher's repertoire. So as a beginning teacher, Sarah took it as the natural order of things that she should ask questions of her practice. Melrose was the ideal setting in which to apply what she was learning to a real-life problem in a school. Sarah began to research her own class as a second-year teacher. She was interested in understanding why some students did not improve in their ability to speak English. She began collecting data in the form of notes she wrote to herself.

Inquiry as an Entry into Leadership

During her third year of teaching, Sarah became a Carnegie scholar. As with Yvonne, the scholars program provided her the opportunity to inquire into her practice more systematically, produce a product, and then make it public for others to see, adapt, and build on. During the Carnegie summer institute, Sarah came to understand that she could represent her inquiry topic through metaphor. She used trains as a way of representing different paths heading for the same destination: learning to speak English. In describing the bilingual students at her school, she explained that one group of students seemed to move seamlessly toward their goal. A second group traveled and made several detours but eventually got to the end of their journey. A third group was constantly derailed and never seemed to achieve their objective. She realized that the practice of grouping students by ability for one hour a day for language development kept the students on the separate trains; one group didn't succeed in learning to speak English.

Sarah had been assigned to teach the lowest-performing group and for most of that time had been troubled by her lack of success. Her inquiry now took the form of a deeper analysis of the data she had collected. She looked at student work, examined report cards, and analyzed the progress of a cohort of eight students over the course of four years. With all this information in hand, Sarah was in a position to create products from her inquiry. She wrote narratives, produced slides, prepared a conference paper, developed a Web site, and made video clips of her classroom. Now she was ready to take her research and its findings to others.

Sarah wanted to use her data to make a case for making fundamental changes in the structure and forms of bilingual instruction, for dismantling the practice of ability grouping for language learning and replacing it with heterogeneous classes. This was no easy task; the school had institutionalized the daily one-hour ability group-ings, and many teachers were convinced that this was a good use of teacher and student time. By now, Sarah had read a great deal. She not only had her own research data to show but also could reference the research of others and demonstrate that the case for heteroge-neous grouping had been made by others. After much discussion, she convinced her colleagues to let her try a pilot project in which the students would be heterogeneously grouped. She agreed to col-lect data on the impact of this form of grouping and report back to the others.

> I structured a new program in which I had a heteroge-
> neous English language development class and organized
> multiple opportunities for students to talk with one
> another in English. The idea guiding this practice was
> that by talking with one another, students could help
> one another learn to speak English. The more experi-
> enced English speakers could assist those less conversant
> and, in doing so, learn more English themselves.
> Throughout the process, I collected various kinds of
> data. . . . I also experimented, using video data to better
> understand what was really going on in my students'
> conversations.

At the end of the year, the data showed that the heteroge-neously grouped students did better than the students who were grouped by ability on a variety of measures in reading, speaking, and conversing in English. Sarah was convinced, but she had to con-vince her colleagues that the change needed to extend beyond her classroom.

She first went public with the information about the success of heterogeneous language development classes to her collaborative inquiry group, where she garnered support for her proposal. She then took her findings, replete with supportive evidence, to the whole school staff. After much discussion, the faculty agreed to change the existing ability grouping for language classes in favor of a heterogeneous approach. A relative tyro had, by dint of research and data collection and analysis, influenced a veteran staff to make a profound change.

Leadership Beliefs and Practices

Sarah's leadership beliefs were shaped by an inquiry process that she initially learned in her master's classes in college. She had the opportunity to extend her research into her school and then to re-fine it during her tenure as a Carnegie scholar. She learned how to go public with her work and how to speak to different audiences based on who they are and their particular interests.

For example, the leadership stance that Sarah takes at her own school is different from the one that she assumes at other schools. She has become aware that sharing knowledge within one's own school is difficult and that she must be careful not to alienate people by coming across as too intellectual or too cocky about her own practice. The egalitarian ethic, which assumes that everyone is the same and that no teacher has more authority than another, as well as other teachers' strong resistance to being told what to do and how to improve, make leadership in one's own school fragile and subtle. Respect, trust, and legitimacy must be developed over time, so that teachers will listen to the messenger. At Melrose, Sarah knew how to work with diverse groups and constituencies and how to build on the culture of teacher research to accomplish her goals.

With audiences outside her school, Sarah advocates strongly for teachers to be thoughtful about their practice by doing research. She makes it clear that she sees teacher research as an effective way to learn to become a better teacher. Her message is not "Do what I do" but rather "Open yourself up to learning by doing your own research." She models her process for others, describing how she went about asking a question, how it haunted her as she continued to collect data, and how she let her inquiry lead her and others to the conclusion that both the structure and the strategies that she and the school were using needed to be changed. She demonstrates how her research helped clarify some areas of her teaching and ask new questions of her practice. This is a powerful message for her to convey to teachers who are struggling with similar problems. Sarah exemplifies how, in its best sense, leadership by inquiry can lead to school reform.

Outside her school, Sarah has presented to enthusiastic audiences. She has led a session entitled "The Impact of Teacher Research on School Policy: One Case Example" at a small schools conference. In a master's class at Mills College, she has shared her inquiry journey with the class, demonstrating how her inquiry has helped her constantly assess where the students are and how (or if) they are learning. At another school, Sarah and her colleagues in the English language development inquiry group presented to other teachers, with Sarah leading discussion on school structure and how it affects student achievement. She has also presented her work at a support group meeting for teachers associated with the National Board of Professional Teaching Standards. She was enthusiastically received, both because of her dogged work on inquiring into her own bilingual classroom and because of her humility and struggle. She made the research process palpable, interesting, engaging, and authentic. Sarah presents herself as an inveterate learner; she inspires others to emulate her inquiry and to identify with her questions about teaching.

In important ways, Sarah is learning how to nuance her message and how to draw from her own work in different contexts. At times, her central message is that her research questions have become a part of her practice. At other times, it focuses on having a good question or on the use of particular data sources (such as video clips) to focus her inquiry on students. Sarah comes across as totally authentic, honest, and open about her struggles as a novice teacher but also as someone who is intelligent, thoughtful, and respectful of her students and the other teachers whom she addresses.

Leadership as Inquiry, Inquiry as Leadership

During the past year, Sarah has become excited about using video to better understand the strategies, problems, and successes her students are having with learning to read, speak, and write in English. In her presentations to teachers, she has added a new topic: the significance of using video to discover how students learn. (See Sarah's Web site at http://kml.carnegiefoundation.org/gallery/scapitelli/index.html.)

> As a teacher researcher who is new to using video in her classroom, I have come to see video as an inquiry tool for both the students and myself that provides the class with new windows through which to reflect upon English language learning and teaching.

Like Yvonne, Sarah has her own Web site; it contains a series of video clips that demonstrate her classroom strategies and the impact of those strategies on her students. This has become more grist for Sarah's mill. She shows video clips to other teachers in her presentations and engages them in the problems of bilingual classrooms, questions of pedagogy, and strategies for student learning. She has also influenced Melrose teachers to use video as a source of achievement data.

This is very powerful leadership from a teacher who has only been teaching for five years. With no formal roles, Sarah leads as a colleague struggling with many of the same problems as her peers. She is willing to go public with her practice, her questions, her data, and her strategies for inquiring into what is going on in her classroom. Teachers find such openness and authenticity attractive and inspiring. They, like Sarah, come to lead by inspiration when they reveal their classrooms to others. And it is her inspiration, rich narratives, and continuing enthusiasm for new techniques (such as video) that leads others to look at their own practice in new ways. Leading for Sarah is informal, collegial, and focused on inquiry. She clearly demonstrates to others what inquiry can yield when teachers make it a part of their teaching, personal growth, and continual professional learning (Eiler-White, 2004).

Leading in Maine

Maine could hardly be more different from California. It is a small, mostly rural state whose entire student population would fill only a small portion of the seats in the Los Angeles County schools. Most of the population is white, with small immigrant populations just now entering the larger cities and towns. Because the long-established trades in manufacturing and the woods are fast disappearing, the state is trying to figure out how to shape a new economy and continue its cherished traditions. Maine is a local control state, where town meetings determine most aspects of civic life and where state mandates are shaped to accommodate local autonomy. Three initiatives, though not as restrictive as those promulgated in California, have had major impacts on the work life of teachers in the public schools and have set the stage for teacher leadership in the state.

- Local accountability and assessment systems are part of state statute. Unlike other states, Maine leaves decisions about who will be promoted and who will graduate to local school boards. While the legislature has adopted a set of learning results to guide district and school planning, it has not mandated a state curriculum or high-stakes test. Rather, each district is expected to develop a local assessment system to measure progress on the learning results. A large proportion of teacher time and energy has been devoted to developing home-grown assessment and accountability systems.

- The Maine Learning Technology Initiative is an ambitious, large-scale attempt to employ computers in classrooms. Its stated goal is to "transform Maine into the premiere state for utilizing technology in kindergarten to grade 12 education in order to prepare students for a future economy that will rely heavily on technology and innovation" (Lane, 2001, p. vi). The strategy is to equip every seventh and eight grader in the state and their teachers with laptop computers, beginning in 2002.

- *Promising Futures: A Call to Improve Learning for Maine's Secondary Students* (Maine Commission on Secondary Education, 1998) is a blueprint for secondary school reform in Maine. Produced by Maine educators and published in 1998, it supports practices that promote rigor, equity, and personalization for all students. In 2003, the Bill and Melinda Gates Foundation funded the Great Maine Schools Project, which works from the document to transform the landscape of secondary education in the state. The project employs three strategies: grants to schools, statewide networking, and public engagement.

This is the context for Gerry Crocker and David Galen, two teachers with multiple and varied school experiences who have become leaders as well as teachers and are helping their colleagues to fulfill the expectations of the state without losing the autonomy that teachers in Maine have long enjoyed.

Gerry Crocker: Linking Vision, Beliefs, and Practice

Gerry Crocker has been teaching and leading in Maine for twenty years. A vocal proponent of *Promising Futures*, she has been a high school science teacher, a school librarian and media specialist, a curriculum and assessment coordinator, a lead teacher in dismantling ability grouping at one high school, and a founding faculty member of another, where heterogeneous grouping was built into the design. As a school librarian, Gerry created the information literacy center at the new school and helped prepare teachers to incorporate information literacy and computer literacy into their teaching repertoire. She has also been a teacher educator and served as a content leader in the Maine Learning Technology Initiative. Currently, Gerry is a coach to four schools in the Great Maine Schools Project.

Gerry came somewhat late to teaching. The daughter of working-class parents, she was told at any early age that college was not something for girls. Although she was in the top ten of her class, she did not apply to college; instead, she entered the workforce. After spending time as a waitress and in cross-country travel, she decided that she wanted more for herself. She won full grant funding to college, where she majored in hydrology. She graduated at the age of twenty-nine and took a job at an engineering firm. After a year, she asked herself, "What am I doing?" and enrolled in the Live, Learn, and Teach program at the University of New Hampshire. The entire program was, in her words, "geared to learning by doing and was all about Dewey."

Beliefs About Teaching and Vision of Schooling

Gerry has held fast to the vision of education she encountered in Live, Learn, and Teach and has continually searched for ways to enact its principles and practices in her teaching and leadership. The program centered on a ten-credit, seven-week summer experience in which a small group of would-be teachers lived together, alongside their mentors and advisers, in a community that they created together. The group worked as a team, "read and lived John Dewey," went rock climbing and took risks together, prepared their own meals, worked in the surrounding community, and attended classes. Gerry's vision of teaching and schooling took root during that summer:

> In Live, Learn, and Teach I learned some common principles that have shaped my life. I believe that we should start with the end in mind; that is, we have to know

where we are going and be sure to make that clear to our students. I believe that kids are at the center of learning, that my job is to get to know them really well and empower them. As adults, we have to organize school in respectful ways that accept kids where they are and move them forward.

Gerry's early family experience did much to shape her deep commitment to developing schools that respect and acknowledge learners and encourage their potential and aspirations. She resonates with students who become discouraged, because she knows what it is like not to have someone believe in her. Her empathy for teenagers and the lives they lead frames much of her perspective:

The raw, human emotions that teens experience are unique and more intense than you'll ever experience. We have to teach them to cope as well as to learn academic subject matter. This is our job.

For Gerry, heterogeneity in classrooms, the absence of tracking and ability grouping, is the hallmark of a respectful high school. This, coupled with teaching that engages students in challenging materials and scaffolds learning, supports and encourages student success. Gerry also values working within a professional community that fosters collaboration, teaming, honesty, and a commitment to having all students enter a future of promise when they graduate.

My beliefs begin with the simple statement that all kids can learn. This doesn't mean they learn the same thing or in the same way. This is where many people get stuck. I believe that teaching is about unleashing potential, understanding students' talents and strengths, creating places where they can learn and grow, helping them persevere in learning challenging material, getting them to think deeply about issues, helping them learn how to learn and to be resourceful, and know where to find the information they need.

In all of her work as a teacher, librarian, and school and state leader, Gerry has faithfully enacted this set of beliefs.

Leading in Reculturing an Existing School

After spending her first year as a teacher in a conventional and highly tracked high school, Gerry assumed a position as teacher-director of a small public alternative school that was designed to serve alienated adolescents who could not adjust to the regular high school. As teacher-director, Gerry implemented many of the ideas she had learned in Live, Learn, and Teach. She initiated a ropes course, taught students how to participate in and facilitate groups, and worked to help them feel empowered. Although student grade point averages and attendance rates increased, few students actually graduated. Somewhat dismayed, Gerry sought out a teaching position in a public school setting that closely reflected her beliefs and vision.

Noble High School was an exciting place to be in the early 1990s. Located in rural southeastern Maine, it served a white working-class and poor population whose aspirations were low and futures severely limited.

> Noble High School was the first school I had heard of that was trying to put into practice the same tenets I had learned in Live, Learn and Teach. It was going to try to make Dewey live in a large public high school.

Under the direction of a new principal, Pam Fisher, the school was in the midst of rethinking its mission and goals, its structures and norms, its methods and practices.

> Pam had set upon a monumental task. She was also a
> great mentor, always placing articles in our mailboxes
> and encouraging us to think in different ways. She sent
> out an e-mail about the first Fall Forum of the Coalition
> of Essential Schools. I badgered her until she agreed to
> let me accompany her to the conference. After the con-
> ference, I was hooked. I saw a common set of principles
> with Live, Learn, and Teach and felt I had become part
> of a movement.

Gerry became a member of the school's leadership team, which went about the business of changing the tone and texture of the school. Propelled by the urgency of creating better futures for the current generation of students, the team did not wait to get everyone on board.

The principal did a great deal of groundwork in the community, enlisting their support for transforming the school before making any formal proposals. When the team proposed the elimination of tracking, the establishment of grade-level teams, and the shift to a block schedule, it had the backing of the school board and of par-ents. As the new practices were implemented, about a third of the teaching staff chose to leave. Their positions were filled by others who shared the vision of the principal and the leadership team. Graduation rates increased, college acceptances soared, and state test results climbed from the bottom third to the top. In this flurry of change, Gerry took an increasing public leadership role at Noble. She also developed an interest in technology and how it could be used to further her vision of schooling. As a leader in professional development, she worked within the school and across the state as a presenter.

> There's nothing like presenting to help you understand
> what you're doing and why you're doing it. It forced me

to stand up and solidify my belief system. I felt that I really helped people get off the fence and get with the program.

Noble became a code word for radical high school change within the state. Other schools talked about being "Noble-ized" with either fear or anticipation. Gerry became more and more of a spokesperson for the school. She found that much of her strength as a leader came from her honesty and willingness to express doubt and uncertainty.

> We never thought of ourselves as experts. We were always willing to share our failings. You have to talk about your failures, because you're always going to have them.

After a brief sojourn in university administration and teaching and a one-year stint in a traditional school (where, she said, "Everything that I believed was called into question"), Gerry found herself at a turning point in her life and decided to retool herself; she enrolled in a master's program in library and information science.

Leading in Culturing a New School

The call of public schools remained strong for Gerry. Armed with a new degree, she was ready to embrace a new challenge. She found that challenge at Poland Regional High School, a school that was not yet fully constructed and whose culture was being shaped before it opened. Gerry had the luxury of completing her degree and knowing exactly where she would be the next fall.

> I knew in December that I had the job. I got to tailor the rest of my master's program toward creating a high school library and multimedia center with a budget of $232,000. I was involved in the interim leadership team from the beginning and had a lot of input into the whole school.

We were going to put in place all of the best work of the
Coalition of Essential Schools and of *Promising Futures*.

Gerry continued at Poland for four years. There she found the
collegial setting and the shared vision she had imagined since her
days as a student in Live, Learn, and Teach. "It was like a dream,"
she says.

The school that the leadership team designed was very different
from any public school in the state. It was organized into grade-level
teams. All classes were heterogeneously grouped, with an "honors
challenge" available in each class. Every student was a member of
a "roundtable," or advisory group, that met consistently with one
faculty member over four years. This ensured that every teacher
knew a few students very well and that every student had one
teacher who was an ally and an advocate. Traditional letter grades
were replaced by Distinguished, Advanced, and Competent. Students had multiple opportunities to earn a Competent; failure was
not an option. All students completed four years each of English,
math, science, and social science and two years of foreign language,
guaranteeing that they could enter college upon graduation. In
order to graduate, in addition to accumulating the necessary credits, students had to complete a final exhibition, called the "senior
celebration," in which they conducted an in-depth investigation of
a topic of interest and made a public presentation about it. Classes
were usually team-taught; assessments were team-designed. The
school governance structure involved faculty and students in a leadership team that was charged with making and enforcing policies
and procedures.

Gerry assumed many leadership roles at Poland. She was a mentor, known as an "Obi-Wan" to younger teachers, each of whom was
called a "Skywalker." She led in structuring the roundtables and
helped develop the senior celebration. She coordinated the grade-
level teams. Each team had a theme for the year: in ninth grade, it was
community; in tenth, it was gateways toward a portfolio; in eleventh,

it focused on careers and service, and in twelfth, it was all about the celebration. Gerry was one of eight coaches for the "critical friends groups" that were major vehicles for professional development in the school. Like all faculty, she participated in four different Tuesday meetings. The first Tuesday of each month was devoted to full faculty professional development decisions, the second to learning areas, the third to roundtable curriculum, and the fourth to critical friends groups.

When the school was the target of criticism from a small parent group in the community, Gerry participated with other teachers, parents, and administrators in mounting an information campaign that won the confidence of the school board and the town council. The going-to-college rate of students from the community increased from 35 percent to 85 percent in five years.

> Poland Regional High School and I were a perfect match. It was a lot like falling in love. The intensity can't be sustained forever, but it is quite overpowering when you're in the midst of it.

Leading in Technology and Information Literacy

Gerry's interest and expertise in technology provided another warrant for her leadership both within Poland Regional High School and beyond it. She created the information center at the school. This was a place where students and faculty alike learned how to use technology to access information, to perform high-quality investigations and research, and to evaluate materials and resources.

> I believe that textbooks are not the best vehicles for learning. I would rather see kids construct their own "books" from the sources they uncover with the guidance of their teachers and me in the information center. In this way, the students not only gain access to current and accurate information, but they also learn to take control of their learning and to empower themselves as learners.

As director of the information center, Gerry worked collaboratively with teachers to plan small classroom projects as well as the more ambitious senior celebrations. She helped the staff become information literate, so they could help the students. The success of the information center was immediate and lasting; it is still booked every hour of the school day.

When the state began to plan the implementation of the middle school laptop initiative, it tapped Gerry for leadership. With the formal title of "content leader," Gerry assumed a statewide role in helping teachers in language arts and libraries learn how to use laptops effectively in their classrooms. Although she was still located at Poland, Gerry had released time to conduct workshops for middle school teachers. She demonstrated how to access resources on the Web in order to conduct research and create instructional units. She showed how to use technology to teach and reinforce skills and to introduce and elaborate concepts. The results of Gerry's work and that of the other content leaders were impressive. Preliminary data indicate that the project is having a positive effect on student interest, attendance, motivation, school performance, and skills:

> Students have reported using their laptops to research information, complete assignments, create projects, and communicate with teachers and other students. . . . They report an increase in interest in their schoolwork and an increase in the amount of work they do both in and out of school. The nature of student learning in classrooms may also be changing because students have the tools to pursue, organize, analyze, and present information more readily at hand. The classroom atmosphere seems to be shifting from teacher led to more student inspired instruction, with students spontaneously searching out new information using their laptops and openly sharing this knowledge. . . [Lane, 2001, pp. 20–21]

Leading in High School Transformation

Gerry has now embarked on a new journey in leadership. She is one of the coaches for the Great Maine Schools Project and works as a coach with four schools that are striving to enact the principles of *Promising Futures*. Not coincidentally, one of the schools that Gerry coaches is Poland High. As a coach, she travels the state, helping the schools in her charge to personalize education, maintain rigor, and promote equity. She draws on all of her past experience when she meets with school faculty and administrators and assists them in plotting a course that often entails detracking the curriculum, reorganizing the school day, using technology to promote learning, and introducing advisories (in which a small group of students and one teacher meet regularly over the students' four years of high school). Gerry describes her role this way:

> I lend support and help guide teachers in exploring new ideas—some I have experienced and others I have not. I look at a situation without having to live inside of it and can offer an objective viewpoint. Some days, I am a cheerleader. I may work with an individual teacher or with a small group, with the leadership team or the principal. I'll say, "What if . . . ?" Invariably, people will launch themselves. I think what I do most is validate and challenge people in their own educational journey.

In this new role, Gerry has been able to consolidate and use the skills, insights, and knowledge that she has accumulated over the span of her professional life:

> To me, this is the culmination of my career. It brings together all of my skills and then some. I am fascinated by the notion that we can move beyond having isolated islands of reform and develop a statewide movement that

takes hold. And for the first time in my life, I have gained the level of confidence in working with adult learners that I think I need to be a true leader.

David Galin: Leading in the "Middle Space"

David Galin is now in his fifteenth year in public education. For the major portion of that time, he has been an elementary and middle school teacher with a special interest in science and math. For the last five years, he has served in the hybrid role of coordinator of teaching and learning in Falmouth, a suburban district just north of Portland. Working on a teacher contract, David is released from regular classroom responsibilities to lead a variety of development activities in service of the district's efforts to comply with the rules and laws pertaining to Maine's learning results and the local assessment system. He facilitates certification by the National Board of Professional Teaching Standards for teachers in the district and works closely with school administrators to create and sustain internal conditions that support teacher leadership and learning and student success in the face of external expectations. As David is wont to say, he works in the "middle space between teachers and administrators."

Like Gerry, David came to teaching in his late twenties. A philosophy major, he entered a new postbaccalaureate teacher preparation program at the University of Southern Maine that was designed for liberal arts graduates and had an emphasis on literacy. Although David says that it was a "highly erratic experience," the program introduced him to compelling ideas about literacy, human development, and learning. He was especially taken with the ideas and values of one of his instructors in mathematics, an area that would later become a cornerstone of his teaching. Upon graduation, David secured his first teaching position as a fourth-grade teacher at an elementary school in a coastal community.

Beginnings: Teaching and Leading at the Same Time

David considers himself lucky to have landed his first job at Coffin School in Brunswick under the principalship of Gil Peterson, an educator with many years' experience as a classroom teacher and curriculum planner. Peterson had recruited a number of new teachers who, like David, had entered teaching as a second career. He strategically placed the newcomers throughout the school in the hopes that they would generate new ideas from within.

> The more I think about it, the more I realize what a great mentor I had in Gil. He helped me define my job as extending beyond the classroom from the very beginning. He encouraged me to think of myself as a leader, even though I was a new teacher. The first piece of good advice he gave me was to spend my first summer as far away from teaching as possible. So, I went to Costa Rica and learned about the rainforest.

The rainforest experience was serendipitous. It positioned David to assume early leadership in a project that had just been initiated in the district.

The Beacon Schools project was the result of a National Science Foundation grant aimed at improving the teaching of science and math in a collaborative of schools in the region. Because of his knowledge of and firsthand experience with an ecological system, David emerged as a leader in connecting science to the lives of students in his school and district and ultimately in the state. He led in Coffin's development of schoolwide study of the Maine coast.

> It was all about the teachers. Gil never stood up and said "me." He turned over every presentation to the teachers. He allowed ideas to percolate up. And in that environment, teachers would pop in with an idea, bring it to

the table, and we'd all make it happen. A teacher who had not left her classroom or done anything innovative in fifteen years would come in with her Bean boots and we were off to the ocean. It was a very special time, before the standards movement took hold and when teachers could really lead the work because it was really their work.

David remained at Coffin School for several years, then transferred to another school in the Beacon project, where he was not so welcomed as a leader. David moved on to Falmouth Middle School, where he was hired as a sixth-grade science teacher and where he continued to combine teaching and leading. The position was a perfect fit.

I worked alongside a wonderful teacher. We had a common schedule and a common philosophy and a room with an adjoining door. Our philosophy was that kids need to be connected to their place; we designed a unit to explore the woods around the school. We also believed that sixth graders are not little adults; we rejected the idea of a mini–high school, required minimal homework and minimal assessments. We wouldn't think twice about interrupting a lesson to deal with real issues. We fought the suburban paradigm; supported connected, active learning; and we got incredible results.

Although he had no prior history in the district, David quickly achieved recognition as a leader. He became a member of the district's strategic planning committee and a charter representative to a newly formed curriculum, instruction, and assessment committee. This last was a stipendiary position that marked the district's first investment in teacher leadership as a strategy for change. He continued in these roles for two years, until a new position was created that would involve him in the "middle space" between teaching and administration.

Teaching and Leading in a New Role

David assumed the role of coordinator of teaching and learning during his third year in Falmouth. It was fortuitous that Leadership for Tomorrow's Schools was just getting started and that David could enroll in the first cohort. This provided him an opportunity to learn about leadership as he practiced it.

> The experience of LTS made a huge difference. Most important was having the opportunity to share assumptions, develop a common language, be involved in joint inquiry, find a direction for my work in my new role, learn to craft a framework from shared learning, and see how to use existing resources to build capacity to get district work done.

David's new position took him out of the classroom and made him look more like an administrator, leading his teacher colleagues to tease gently that he had "crossed over to the dark side." On the other hand, it planted him even more firmly as a teacher, this time as a teacher of adults.

> This has been the tension for five years. I have had to learn to work in the middle space between teachers and administrators. I have found that I am most effective in doing this when I work in small groups or individually. In a high school meeting, I'll go and present an idea and be met with stony silence. The next day, I'll go and work with an individual, and we'll have a good conversation and make a plan for action. That's how it goes. In large group settings, people see me as an administrator. In a small group or one-on-one, they see me as a resource.

David has come to believe that the role he plays in the district is within the purview of teacher leadership and that a principal cannot do this kind of work, especially in the new era of accountability. He also believes that teacher leadership adds value to the work of the district and makes a significant contribution to school change.

> The teacher leaders I work with meet regularly with the administrative team to learn and plan together. Without fail, those meetings create a much deeper understanding than when either group meets alone. Including teacher leaders in this type of work is one way that a district creates capacity for transformational change.

David's leadership work is quite varied. He coordinates state and federal grants and oversees district professional development for administrators as well as teachers. He has helped create leadership teams in the elementary schools, which allow teachers to take responsibility for all content area work in grades K–2 and grades 3–4. He leads K–12 curriculum development and curriculum mapping and works closely with stipendiary teacher leaders. And David was instrumental in having the district reallocate its professional development funds, increasing the general pool and giving a larger share to the elementary level. That change has "enabled new work to happen," he says. To his mind, his most important responsibilities lie in the areas of local assessment development and facilitation of National Board certification processes.

Local Assessment Development

David is in charge of all curriculum and assessment development to bring the district in line with statutory requirements. This difficult and complex task requires a level of expertise and technical skill greater than that of most teachers; yet the state has made local assessments the hallmark of its strategy, viewing them as a hedge against the standardized measures and standardized means that have been adopted by most other states. David sees his role in all of this as being a translator:

> I see the numbers and the mumbo jumbo, and I try to find clarity. This is a translation process. But it is not a word-for-word translation; I bring my values to it. It is a value-driven translation.

David has been very successful in bringing the Falmouth system up to date with state requirements. The Falmouth template has become an exemplar for many districts in the state and is highlighted in a statewide Web site (www.usm.maine.edu/smp/tools/primer.htm). By inviting, mediating, and guiding teacher involvement, he has made difficult work easier to understand and manage. However, David does not view this effort as exemplary of the kind of teacher leadership he wants to embrace. David's passion in leadership lies elsewhere.

> There is a difference between translating for people and constructing with them. When you co-construct, people own the work. When you translate, they let you own it. They thank you for making the work easier, but the work isn't theirs. I am afraid that this is the way people lose their passion, and that is a great loss. I call it the standards-based loss, and it is something to worry about.

Facilitating National Board Certification

David's position places him in charge of all district professional development. As part of his leadership in this area, he decided to find out about the process of certification for the National Board of Professional Teaching Standards. His district paid for him to attend a training session in Las Vegas, where he learned what the standards entailed, what the process of certification required, and how to work

effectively with teachers toward demonstration. So far, he has provided guidance and support for two groups of teachers who have
gone through the process, and he is about to start work with a new
group. David considers his work in this area to be the most effective professional learning he has experienced and an empowering
form of teacher leadership.

> Leaders have to be grounded in practice; you have to
> come back to it. It's a lens you have to look through—
> staying current with realities of classroom teaching. I do
> the National Board work because it puts me in class-
> rooms. I'm in there videotaping teachers, watching the
> tapes, going over unit and lesson plans. More than any-
> thing else, it has maintained my social capital. I've been
> out of the classroom for five years. This brings me back
> in. It is a true teacher leadership role with major impli-
> cations for improving teaching and learning.

David clearly articulates how the process of preparing teachers
to complete their portfolios for National Board certification is a
model for good professional development:

> It includes small cohorts of teachers working over time
> with each other on a common goal; it allows for unlim-
> ited released time; it allows teachers to work together
> on common pieces; it makes practice more transparent;
> and it makes use of internal and external knowledge and
> connections.

David can also identify why facilitation represents the kind of
teacher leadership he wants to embrace:

> In this context, teachers look at their practice, and they
> improve. There is no other supervision/professional
> development model I've seen that gets people to improve

their practice to the degree that this does. To watch defensive walls break down is very different from watching people use someone else's templates or implement someone else's translation. This is about real ownership and allows teachers to reclaim their passion. It replenishes the standards-based loss.

Platform for Teacher Leadership

David's vision of teacher leadership has deepened over time; it has its roots in his first experience as a teacher under Gil Peterson at Coffin School, where he learned that

> Leadership is about letting go of your authority and letting others in, letting them lead the work. That is the sticking point. That's where you watch people fall out. But for teachers to grow, they have to be able to lead, and you have to not only let it happen, you have to encourage it and fight to maintain it—even when it is easier for you to do things yourself.

David has come to see teacher leadership as being about helping teachers make the transition from looking at curriculum and textbooks to looking at student work and teacher practice and from telling stories and relating anecdotes to looking at data and using them to make decisions about teaching and learning.

David believes that for teacher leadership to be successful, it must have an infrastructure and an investment at the district level. These conditions for success became apparent to him when he enrolled in the Leadership for Tomorrow's Schools program. There he saw a clear difference between participants from districts that had made an investment in teacher leadership and from districts that had not made that investment:

> A few of us became a subcohort within the cohort. We all had released time positions, which was a good indi-

cation of the level of district support. We became a think tank, and we all got smarter exponentially. Some of the other participants didn't have that advantage. Their superintendents said they would lend support, but it was not as strong as it could have been. These people had little opportunity or culture in which to see themselves as leaders. They as much as said, "This will not go anywhere for me."

David is convinced that a large part of his success as a teacher leader in Falmouth is due to the commitment of the district and its willingness to reallocate resources to support a strong teacher leadership structure.

Finally, David has come to view teacher leadership as a necessary but not sufficient element in school transformation:

> Unless you have teacher leadership *and* strong administrative leadership, you don't get to transformation. Teachers and administrators often get into "learned powerlessness," especially when it comes to standards. When a new paradigm is introduced, the default is the known; the instinct is to recreate the second-grade classroom you experienced. It is up to both teacher and administrative leaders to create the conditions that push the conversation beyond blame and helplessness, to create a tone that says, "We're smart enough to make good choices for us and for our students."

Teacher Leadership: From Practice to Theory

In this book, our intent has been to set the context for the emergence of teacher leadership as an important way to deal with the impact of worldwide changes in schools. We have reviewed relevant research and written cases about two communities of practice that have developed ways of creating and supporting teachers as leaders. But it is in the work of Yvonne, Sarah, Gerry, and David that we gain deep understandings of why and how teachers take leadership positions and what they do when they get them. These teacher leaders give us reason to hope in this time of unprecedented change. People like these four deserve to be recognized and supported by others. Teacher leadership is one powerful way to make our schools work for everyone in them—the students and their teachers.

What can we learn from our four exemplars about how to maintain continued optimism and passion for teaching and learning despite frustration and seemingly unsolvable problems? We believe that teachers who lead

- Develop strong commitments to their students through their life experiences and their own teaching

- Become inquirers into their own practice, helping them to become articulate about learning and teaching

- Provide leadership through their example of becoming lifelong learners themselves

- Take risks by expanding their own comfort zones and modeling experimentation

- Inspire their peers through their commitment to continual struggle to improve their practice

- Work hard at expanding their circle of friends and their own knowledge base

- Organize novice and veteran teachers into communities of support

- Care about the content and character of colleagueship as well as the content of the subject matter

- Learn to lead through colleagueship and humility

- Create incentives for themselves and others to understand that learning to teach is a lifetime affair within a community of learners

- Understand that sensitivity to context and culture is a critical part of leadership

- Find a variety of opportunities to lead and keep learning

- Go public with their understandings about students, strategies for learning, and the organization of the curriculum

- Pursue improvement despite negative responses to change

When teachers lead, they help to create an environment for learning that influences the entire school community. Beginning teachers find sympathetic and knowledgeable colleagues to work with, examples of practice to emulate, and habits of inquiry that will last throughout their career. Veteran teachers open up to issues outside their classroom that affect what goes on inside; they find new reasons to share their hard-earned knowledge and identify with a larger community. These kinds of changes shape the school community—indeed, make it more of a learning community—leading to the recruitment and retention of more and better novice teachers, invigorating the professional lives of experienced teachers, and raising the quality of teaching and learning for both students and their teachers.

This is not to say that being a teacher leader is easy. We do not mean to imply that teacher leadership is fully integrated into the teaching culture, nor do we want to gloss over the difficulties that await professionals who seek to change the very concept of what it means to be a teacher. Change is always accompanied by conflict, disequilibrium, and confusion. In the current era, shaped as it is by dramatic changes in the world and dominated by a push toward accountability and standardization, change that calls for the development of communities may be even more difficult to achieve and maintain.

Despite all of this, our study of teacher leadership imbues us with hope; it helps us envision a future in which teachers lead toward more democratic and enlightened schooling. The teacher leaders we have come to know are committed for the long term; they do not intend to give up on their students or one another. They plan to continue to assume responsibility for the deepening of their own practice and that of their colleagues. They are determined to become the architects of vibrant professional communities in which teachers take the lead in inventing new possibilities for their students and for themselves.

References

Bartlett, L. (2001). *A question of fit: Conceptions of teacher role and conditions of teacher commitment*. Unpublished doctoral dissertation, University of California, Berkeley.

Carnegie Corporation of New York. (1986). *A nation prepared: Teachers for the twenty-first century*. New York: Author.

Cochran-Smith, M., & Lytle, S. (1993). Teacher research: A way of knowing. In M. Cochran-Smith & S. Lytle (Eds.), *Inside/outside: Teacher research and knowledge* (pp. 41–62). New York: Teachers College Press.

Cochran-Smith, M., & Lytle, S. (2001). Beyond certainty: Taking an inquiry stance on practice. In *Teachers caught in the action: Professional development that matters* (pp. 45–56). New York: Teachers College Press.

Cuban, L. (1990). A fundamental puzzle of school reform. In A. Lieberman (Ed.), *Schools as collaborative cultures*. New York: Falmer Press.

Darling-Hammond, L. (1991). The implications of testing policy for quality and equality. *Kappan, 73*(3), 220–225.

Darling-Hammond, L., & McLaughlin, M. W. (1983). Investing in teaching as a learning profession: Policy, problems and prospects. In L. Darling-Hammond & G. Sykes (Eds.), *Teaching as the learning profession: Handbook of policy and practice* (pp. 376–411). New York: Longman.

Eiler-White, M. (2004). *Going public. The representation and travel of teacher research*. Unpublished doctoral dissertation, Stanford University.

Fullan, M. (1994). Teacher leadership: A failure to conceptualize. In D. R. Walling (Ed.), *Teachers as leaders: Perspectives on the professional development of teachers* (pp. 241–253). Bloomington, IN: Phi Delta Kappa Educational Foundation.

Fullan, M. (1995, November). *Broadening the concept of teacher leadership*. Paper presented at the National Staff Development Council, New Directions Conference, Chicago, Ill.

Gawande, A. (2002). *Complications: A surgeon's notes on an imperfect science.* New York: Henry Holt.

Giddens, A. (2003). *Runaway world: How globalization is reshaping our lives.* New York: Routledge.

Gray, J. (2000). *Teaching at the center: A memoir of the early years of the National Writing Project.* Berkeley, CA: National Writing Project.

Grossman, P., Wineburg, S., & Woolworth, S. (2001, December). Toward a theory of teacher community. *Teachers College Record, 103,* 942–1012.

Hargreaves, A. (1994). *Changing teachers, changing times: Teachers' work and culture in the postmodern age.* New York: Teachers College Press.

Hargreaves, A. (2003). *Teaching in the knowledge society: Education in the age of insecurity.* New York: Teachers College Press.

Hatch, T., Eiler, M., & Faigenbaum, D. (2003). *Expertise, credibility, and influence: How teachers change the system.* Unpublished paper, Carnegie Foundation for the Advancement of Teaching, Stanford, CA.

Hodgkinson, H. (2001). Educational demographics: What teachers should know. *Educational Leadership, 58*(14), 6–11.

Huberman, M. (1993). *The lives of teachers.* New York: Teachers College Press.

Hutchinson, Y. D. (2003). *A friend of their minds: Capitalizing on the oral tradition of my African American students.* Retrieved April 5, 2004 from http://gallery.carnegiefoundation.org/yhutchinson

Lambert, L. (2003). Shifting conceptions of leadership: Towards a redefinition of leadership for the twenty-first century. In B. Davies & J. West-Burnham (Eds.), *Handbook of educational leadership and management* (pp. 5–15). London: Pearson Education.

Lane, D.M.M. (2001). *Early evidence from the field. The Maine learning technology initiative: Impact on students and learning.* Occasional paper no. 1. Gorham, ME: Center for Educational Policy, Applied Research and Evaluation, University of Southern Maine.

Lave, J. (1996). Teaching, as learning: In practice. *Mind, Culture and Activity, 3*(3), 149–164.

Lave, J., & Wenger, E. (1991). *Situated learning: Legitimate peripheral participation.* Cambridge, UK: Cambridge University Press.

Lieberman, A. (1991). Accountability as a reform strategy. *Kappan, 73*(3), 219–220.

Lieberman, A., & Miller L. (1992). *Teachers, their world and their work.* New York: Teachers College Press.

Lieberman, A., & Miller, L. (1999). *Teachers—transforming their world and their work.* New York: Teachers College Press.

Lieberman, A., & Miller, L. (2000). Teaching and teacher development: A new synthesis for a new century. In R. S. Brandt (Ed.), *Education in a new era* (pp. 47–63). Alexandria, VA: Association for Supervision and Curriculum Development.

Lieberman, A., & Wood, D. (2003). *Inside the National Writing Project: Connecting network learning with classroom teaching.* New York: Teachers College Press.

Little, J. W. (1990). Teachers as colleagues. In A. Lieberman, (Ed.), *Schools as collaborative cultures* (pp. 165–193). New York: Falmer Press.

Little, J. W. (1995). Contested ground: The basis of teacher leadership in two restructuring high schools. *Elementary School Journal, 96*(1), 47–63.

Little, J. W., & Bartlett, L. (2002). Career and commitment in the context of comprehensive school reform. *Theory and Practice, 8*(3), 345–354.

Maine Commission on Secondary Education. (1998). *Promising Futures: A Call to Improve Learning for Maine's Secondary Students.* Augusta, Maine: Maine Department of Education.

Mazar, M. J. (1997). *Global trends 2005: An owner's manual for the next decade.* New York: St. Martin's Press.

McLaughlin, M. W., & Talbert, J. (1993). *Contexts that matter for teaching and learning.* Stanford, CA: Context Center for Teaching and Learning in Secondary Schools.

Miles, M., Saxl, E., & Lieberman, A. (1988). What skills do educational "change agents" need? An empirical view. *Curriculum Inquiry, 18*(2), 157–193.

Miller, L., & O'Shea, C. (1991). Learning to lead. In A. Lieberman (Ed.), *The changing contexts of teaching* (pp. 197–211). Chicago: University of Chicago Press.

Moore, M. (2004). *The role of legitimate peripheral participation in school leader preparation* (working title). Unpublished doctoral dissertation, University of Maine, Orono.

National Commission on Excellence in Education. (1983). *A nation at risk: The imperative for educational reform.* Washington, DC: U.S. Department of Education.

Ohanian, S. (1999). *One size fits few: The folly of educational standards.* Portsmouth, NH: Heinemann Educational Books.

Polanyi, M. (1967). *The tacit dimension.* London: Routledge.

Rogoff, B. (1994, Fall). Developing understanding of the idea of communities of learners. *Mind, Culture and Activity, 1*(4), 209–229.

Schön, D. (1983). *The reflective practitioner: How professionals think in action.* New York: Basic Books.

Schön, D. (1991). *The reflective turn: Case studies in and on educational practice.* New York: Teachers College Press.

Seely Brown, J. (1998). Research that reinvents the corporation. In *Harvard Business Review on knowledge management* (pp. 153–180). Cambridge, MA: Harvard Business School Press.

Shulman, L. (2000). From Minsk to Pinsk: Why a scholarship of teaching and learning? *Journal of Scholarship of Teaching, 1*(1), 48–52.

Smylie, M. A. (1995). New perspectives on teacher leadership. *Elementary School Journal,* 96(1), 3–63.

Smylie, M. A., & Denny, J. W. (1990, August). Teacher leadership: Tensions and ambiguities in organizational perspective. *Educational Administration Quarterly, 26*(3), 235–259.

Spillane, J. P., Hallett, T., & Diamond, J. B. (2003). Forms of capital and the construction of leadership: Leadership in urban elementary schools. *Sociology of Education, 76*(1).

Stern, S. (2003, October 7). The great escape. *Christian Science Monitor,* p. 1.

Strong, M., & St. John, L. (in press). *Research working paper no. 3.* Santa Cruz, CA: Santa Cruz New Teacher Program.

Wasley, P. (1991). *Teachers who lead: The rhetoric of reform and the realities of practice.* New York: Teachers College Press.

Wenger, E. (1998). *Communities of practice: Learning, meaning, and identity.* Cambridge, U.K.: Cambridge University Press.

Westheimer, J. (1998). *Among schoolteachers: Community, autonomy, and ideology in teachers' work.* New York: Teachers College Press.

Wood, D., & Lieberman, A. (2000). Teachers as authors: The National Writing Project's approach to professional development. *International Journal of Leadership in Education, 3*(3), 255–273.

Zumwalt, K., & Craig, E. (in press). Demographic profile. In M. C. Smith & K. Zeichner (Eds.), *The report of the AERA Panel on Research and Teacher Education.* Washington, DC: American Educational Research Association.

Index

Robert J. Starratt
ETHICAL LEADERSHIP

In *Ethical Leadership*, Robert Starratt—one of the leading thinkers on the topic of ethics and education—shows educational leaders how to move beyond mere technical efficiency in the delivery and performance of learning. He challenges educators to become ethical leaders who understand the learning process as a profoundly moral activity that engages the full humanity of the school community.

ISBN 0-7879-6564-2   Paperback   160 Pages (approx.)   Summer 2004

James Ryan
INCLUSIVE LEADERSHIP

The culture of schools and the diversity of those who lead them have not kept pace with the growing diversity in the student population. The culture of today's school is often "Balkanized"—making effective leadership a particular challenge. James Ryan's work focuses on leadership as an intentionally inclusive practice that values all cultures and all types of students in a school. This book draws on his groundbreaking research to develop the powerful new idea of inclusive leadership.

ISBN 0-7879-6508-1   Paperback   128 Pages (approx.)   2005

James Spillane
DISTRIBUTIVE LEADERSHIP

"Distributive Leadership" is a new concept in education—the ways in which leadership is exercised in everyday practice through communications and actions, and via others in the school community such as teachers and parents. In this book, James Spillane, the leading expert on "Distributive Leadership," explores the distribution of leadership among various people in the school, and the extent to which leadership is stretched over tools and physical materials in the organization such as memos, scheduling procedures, evaluation protocols, computer programs, and more.

ISBN 0-7879-6538-3   Paperback   128 Pages (approx.)   2005

Michael Fullan
TURNAROUND LEADERSHIP
ISBN 0-7879-6985-0
Paperback
128 Pages (approx.)
2005

Andy Hargreaves, Dean Fink
SUSTAINING LEADERSHIP
ISBN 0-7879-7277-0
Paperback
128 Pages (approx.)
2005

Geoffrey Southworth
LEARNER-CENTERED LEADERSHIP
ISBN 0-7879-7553-2
Paperback
128 Pages (approx.)
2005